ISSN 0177-1647

BULLETIN
OF THE
MIDDLE EASTERN CULTURE CENTER IN JAPAN

General Editor: H. I. H. Prince Takahito Mikasa

Vol. I

MONARCHIES AND SOCIO-RELIGIOUS TRADITIONS IN THE ANCIENT NEAR EAST

(Papers read at the 31st International Congress of Human Sciences in Asia and North Africa)

Edited by

H. I. H. Prince Takahito Mikasa

1984

OTTO HARRASSOWITZ · WIESBADEN

MONARCHIES AND SOCIO-RELIGIOUS TRADITIONS IN THE ANCIENT NEAR EAST

(Papers read at the 31st International Congress of Human Sciences in Asia and North Africa)

Edited by

H. I. H. Prince Takahito Mikasa

1984
OTTO HARRASSOWITZ · WIESBADEN

The *Bulletin of the Middle Eastern Culture Center in Japan* is published by Otto Harrassowitz on behalf of the Middle Eastern Culture Center in Japan.

CIP-Kurztitelaufnahme der Deutschen Bibliothek

Monarchies and socio-religious traditions in the ancient Near East :
papers read at the 31st Internat. Congress of Human Sciences in Asia and North Africa /
ed. by Prince Takahito Mikasa. – Wiesbaden : Harrassowitz, 1985.
(Bulletin of the Middle Eastern Culture Center in Japan ; Vol. 1)
ISBN 3-447-02510-7
NE: Mikasa, Takahito ⟨Prinz⟩ [Hrsg.]; International Congress of Human Sciences
in Asia and North Africa ⟨31, 1983, Tōkyō⟩

Phototypesetting, reproduction and binding:
MZ-Verlagsdruckerei GmbH, Memmingen
Printed in Germany

CONTENTS

PREFACE

The papers presented here were delivered on 1st September, 1983 to the Ancient Near and Middle East section (Section 2) of the XXXIst International Congress of Human Sciences in Asia and North Africa held in Tokyo, Japan. I had the pleasure of being Honorary President on that occasion which was noteworthy in that it was the first meeting of the Congress (formerly the International Congress of Orientalists) to take place in the Far East and the first gathering there to draw scholars specialising in the ancient Near East from many countries.

Further papers on this region, primarily those on archaeology, were read to other Sections of the same meeting. Abstracts of these, as of all, papers have been published in the official volumes of the Proceedings.

The Middle Eastern Culture Center in Japan, as one of the major organisers and supporters of the Congress, considered that these papers warranted a fuller and wider publication since they contributed to areas of study which are among its own major research interests. The title reflects a theme on which papers were invited initially. Inevitably, however, only some aspects of such a wide-ranging and influential subject which dominates the culture of the ancient Near East could be offered. Nevertheless, they include contributions on aspects of historical, religious, social and cultural significance. Thus they are made available as a help to ongoing specialist studies in Egyptology, Assyriology, Old Testament and related disciplines, to which Japanese scholars increasingly bring their distinctive interpretations. No attempt has been made to impose any uniformity of style or reference where clarity is not impaired and the terminology and abbreviations are readily familiar to students in the respective areas of study.

Prince Takahito Mikasa

L. M. MUNTINGH (University of Stellenbosch)

THE CONCEPTION OF ANCIENT SYRO-PALESTINIAN KINGSHIP IN THE LIGHT OF CONTEMPORARY ROYAL ARCHIVES WITH SPECIAL REFERENCE TO THE RECENT DISCOVERIES AT TELL MARDIKH (EBLA) IN SYRIA.*

Introduction

Henri Frankfort commences his classical book *Kingship and the gods. A study of Ancient Near Eastern Religion as the integration of society and nature* (1948) by stating that the ancient Near East considered kingship the very basis of civilization. A purely secular approach to kingship was hardly possible. However, because of their attitudes towards nature, Egypt and Mesopotamia, the two centres of ancient civilization, held very different views in connection with kingship. In both countries the people regarded the king as their mediator with the gods, but in Mesopotamia the king was only the foremost citizen (Sumerian lugal, "great man"), while in Egypt, the Pharaoh (*pr-* ᶜ³, "great house") was a divine descendant of the gods (pp. 3ff.).

In his epilogue (pp. 337ff.) Frankfort discusses a third kind of kingship in the ancient Near East. In addition to the god incarnate, who was Pharaoh and the chosen servant of the gods who ruled Mesopotamia, we find a hereditary leader whose authority derived from descent and originally was coextensive with kingship; *inter alia* in Syria and in Palestine where the Hebrews lived. As a result of the fact that the Hebrew prophets rejected both the Egyptian and the Babylonian views and insisted on the uniqueness and transcendence of God, both kingship and nature were secularized. Thus, says Frankfort, kingship is bereft of a function which it exercised all through the Near East, where its principal task lay in the maintenance of harmony with the gods in nature.

In the light of Frankfort's approach we shall try, by means of texts from contemporary royal archives and the Old Testament, to determine the conception of kingship in ancient Syria and Palestine. Although our sources cover a period of ± 1800 years they have at least two common characteristics; *geographically* (the Syro-Palestinian peoples lived in adjoining countries) and *linguistically*

* A grant by the Human Sciences Research Council, Pretoria, Republic of South Africa, to attend the XXXI CISHAAN is acknowledged with gratitude.

(the people were of Amorite-Canaanite origin and they spoke North-west Semitic languages).

1 *Ebla*

The archives, found in the Royal Palace at Tell Mardikh, the ancient Ebla, in Northern Syria during excavations in 1974–76 consist of the records of a previously unknown kingdom that flourished approximately 2400 BC.[1] A new chapter has been added to Protosyrian history of the third millennium BC.[2] Ebla was finally identified with Tell Mardikh by means of the inscribed statue of king Ibbit-Lim who ruled at Ebla around 2000 BC, and who wrote his dedication to the goddess Ishtar in the Akkadian language.[3]

Hundreds of geographical names are revealed in the texts and we now realize how vast the empire of Ebla, that controlled all Syria-Palestine to the south and other areas, was.[4] She had contact with cultural centres such as Kish[5], Abu Salabikh[6], Mari[7] and Egypt[8]. The empire of Ebla was founded on her economy that was essentially a state economy in which the role of the king was decisive.[9]

1 G. Pettinato, "Gli archivi reali di Tell Mardikh-Ebla. Riflessioni e prospettive", *RBI* 25 (1977) p. 233; *The Archives of Ebla, an empire inscribed in clay*, 1981 (abbreviated *Ebla*), p. 72, dates the archives ± 2500 BC. For a later date, however, see A. Archi, "A mythologem in Eblaitology: Mesilim of Kish at Ebla", *Studi Eblaiti* (= *SEb*) IV 1981, p. 229.

2 P. Matthiae, *Ebla, an empire rediscovered*, 1979.

3 G. Pettinato, "Inscription de Ibbit-Lim, roi de Ebla", *AAAS* 20 (1970), pp. 73–76; *RBI* 25 (1977), pp. 226–227; *Ebla* pp. 23–28; M. Heltzer, "The inscription from Tell-Mardiḫ and the city Ebla in northern Syria in the III–II millennium BC", *AION* 25 (1977), pp. 291 ff. Heltzer dates the inscription between 2123 and 2047 BC (p. 31). The language of the inscription is (Old-) Akkadian; see Heltzer, p. 317, and G. Garbini, "Considerations on the language of Ebla", in L. Cagni (editor), *La lingua di Ebla*. Instituto Universitario Orientale Seminario di Studi Asiatici. Series Minor XIV, Naples 1981 (abbreviated *IUO XIV*), p. 78.

4 G. Pettinato, "L'Atlante geografico del Vicino Oriente Antico attestato ad Ebla e ad Abu Ṣalabikh (I)", *Or NS* 47 (1978), pp. 50–73; *Ebla*, pp. 96, 241.

5 I. J. Gelb, "Ebla and the Kish Civilization", *IUO XIV*, pp. 9–73 ("After the great discoveries at Ebla we are slowly getting acquainted with the Syrian side of the Kish Civilization . . .", p. 73); A. Archi, "Kish nei testi di Ebla", *SEb* IV 1981, pp. 77–87.

6 R. D. Biggs, "Ebla and Abu Salabikh: the linguistic and literary aspects" *IUO XIV*, pp. 121–133.

7 G. Pettinato, "Relations entre les royaumes d'Ebla et de Mari au troisieme millenair d'apres les Archives Royales de Tell Mardikh-Ebla", *Akkadica* 2, (1977), pp. 20–28; A. Archi, "I rapporti tra Ebla e Mari", *SEb* IV 1981, pp. 129–166.

8 G. S. Matthiae, "Vasi iscritti de Chefren e Pepi I nel Palazzo Reale G di Ebla", *SEb* I 1979, pp. 33–43; "Un oggetto faraonico della XIII dinastia dalla 'Tomba del Signore dei capridi'", *ibid.*, pp. 119–128.

9 Pettinato, *Ebla*, pp. 179 ff.

1.1 Sources

The sources for our study, which come from the royal archives of Ebla, are the administrative texts[10], bilingual texts with Sumerian-Eblaic lexical lists[11], as well as letters and treaties.

The study of Eblaic is still in its infancy as E. Sollberger has correctly stated.[12] The language of Ebla, for the first time identified by G. Pettinato, the epigraphist, and classified as North-west Semitic and named Old-Canaanite[13], is a subject of intensive study as is well reflected in the published account of the international conference on the language of Ebla held in Naples in 1980.[14] Formerly Pettinato estimated that 80% of the Ebla texts had been written in Sumerian and 20% in Eblaic[15], but in later years he changed his mind on this matter and assumed that the bilingualism of the tablets is only apparent. The Sumerian terms are in reality logograms and all of them were read in Eblaic, he says.[16] I. J. Gelb is also of the opinion that the great majority of the Ebla texts were written in the Eblaic language, not in Sumerian.[17]

1.2 Terms for "King" and "Kingship" in the Ebla Texts

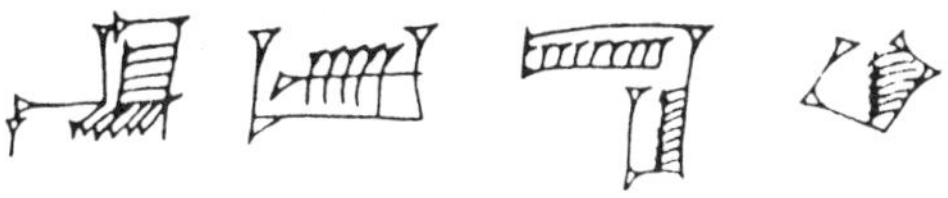

EN EB LA KI

"King of Ebla"

10 See G. Pettinato, *Catalogo dei testi cuneiformi di Tell Mardikh-Ebla*, Materiali epigrafici di Ebla – 1 (= MEE 1), Naples 1979; *Testi amministrativi della biblioteca L. 2769*, Parte 1, MEE 2, Naples 1980; D. O. Edzard, *Verwaltungstexte verschiedenen Inhalts (aus dem Archiv L. 2769)* Archivi Reali di Ebla. Testi – II (ARET II) Rome 1981; A. Archi and M. G. Biga, *Testi amministrativi di vario contenuto* (Archivio L. 2769: TM.75.G.3000–4101), ARET III, Rome 1982. Before the official publication of the texts some of them were already published and discussed in various journals.

11 See G. Pettinato, "I vocabolari bilingui di Ebla. Problemi di traduzioni e di lessicografia Sumerico-Eblaita" *IUO XIV*, pp. 241–276; G. Pettinato, in collaboration with E. Arcari, A. Magi-Spinetti and G. Visicato, *Testi lessicali bilingui della Biblioteca L. 2769.* Parte I: *Traslitterazione dei testi e riconstruzione del VE* (MEE 4), Naples 1982.

12 *SEb* III/9–10 1980, p. 132.

13 "Testi cuneiforme del 3. millennio in paleo-cananeo rinvenuti nella campagna 1974 a Tell Mardikh=Ebla", *Or NS* 44 (1975), pp. 361–374.

14 Published in *IUO XIV* (cf. n. 3 above).

15 *RBI* 25 (1977), p. 238.

16 *Ebla*, p. 57.

17 *IUO XIV*, pp. 11, 13.

The four cuneiform signs, reproduced here, in the writing of the Eblaites were important for the historic identification of Tell Mardikh with Ebla.[18] The Sumerian logogram en is the only indication for "king" in the archives of Ebla, but then not only for the king of Ebla. Quite a number of toponyms in the texts are followed by en[19], thus the cuneiform phrase en *-eb-la*^{ki}, "king of Ebla" is the only real indication that someone was the king of Ebla. The logogram en appears in various combinations.[20]

The Sumerian en is rendered *m(ā)likum* in the bilingual vocabularies.[21] The construct state ends in ∅: *ma-lik* GN/ *malik* GN/ "king of GN" while instances of the misuse of the case are found in *ma-lik-tum*.[22] The phonetic manner of writing, namely *malikum* is well attested in numerous personal names with the theophorous element *ma-lik*, being the name of Malik, one of the most popular gods in Ebla. An analogous manner of writting appears in a bilingual text where nam.en = *ma-lī-gú-um* (TM.75.G.2001+2003 v. XI:11 f.), clearly from the root *mlk*. The problem is, however, that *ma-lī-gú-um* does not represent the Eblaic word for "king" as the Sumerian equivalent has the meaning "kingship". Substantives of the type 1a2ī3 (hence/*malīk-um*/) are abstracts in Akkadian, Hebrew and Arabic. In the same bilingual list Sumerian nam.nam.en is translated *du-da-li-gú-um* (v.IX:13 f.) to be understood as /*tumtallik-um*/, "to exercise the kingship", a verbal abstract of the Dt form of **mlk* with the total assimilation of *m* to the following dental *-t*.[23] While Fronzaroli understands *du-da-lī-gú-um* as *tumtallikum*, M. Dahood normalizes the former as *tu-da-ri-ku-um*, since *li* often stands for *ri* in the Ebla texts. The concurrence of the synonymous roots *mlk* and *drk* in the same bilingual text is later continued in the poetic pair *mlk*, "kingship" //*drkt*, "dominion" in Ugaritic and still later in Biblical Hebrew.[24]

It seems to me that Pettinato does not make a distinction between *mālikum*, "king" and *malīkum*, "kingship". He gives as one example from the bilingual vocabularies nam – en = *ma-li-ku-um (mlk)* "king".[25] Elsewhere he states that the Sumerian equivalent of *malikum*, "king" is not en, but rather nam–en which means, however, "kingship". Dahood adds to this remark that it explains

18 Pettinato, *Ebla*, pp. 7–8, 35.

19 Pettinato, MEE 2, p. 354; Archi-Biga, ARET *III*, p. 348.

20 See Edzard, ARET II, p. 123, and Archi-Biga, ARET III, pp. 347–48. Edzard: en = "'Herrscher' (konventionelle Übersetzung").

21 G. Pettinato, *RBI* 25 (1977), p. 240: en = *ma-li-ku$_8$-um*, "king"; *Ebla*, p. 74; cf. p. 62.

22 Gelb, *IUO XIV*, p. 32, who refers to Pettinato, MEE I, p. 274.

23 P. Fronzaroli, "Un atto reale di donazione dagli Archivi di Ebla (TM.75.G.1766)", *SEb* I/1 1979, pp. 5–6; A. Archi, "Les textes lexicaux bilingues d'Ebla", *SEb* II/6 1980, p. 86.

24 "The linguistic classification of Eblaite", *IUO XIV*, pp. 188–189. For the god Malik in theophorous names see Pettinato, *Ebla*, p. 260.

25 "The royal archives of Tell Mardikh-Ebla", *BA* 39/2 (1976), p. 50.

why the word for "king" in Phoenician is the abstract form ממלכת and why in Biblical Hebrew ממלכה in a number of texts (e.g. 1 Sam 10:18; Ps 68:33, means "king".[26] J. Friedrich, on the contrary, explains the Phoenician-Punic ממלכת, "kingship" > "king" (*mamlakūt* or *mamlakōt*?); cf. Hebrew ממלכות and ממלכה.[27]

The whole position may be summarized as follows:

SUMERIAN	EBLAIC	HEBREW	PHOENICIAN
en, "king"	*mālikum*	מלך	מלך
nam.en	*malīkum* /	ממלכות /	ממלכת
"kingship"	*ma-li-gú-um*	ממלכה	(**mamlakūt*
			**mamlakōt*?)

In Ebla the feminine of *mālikum*, "king" was *māliktum*, "queen" (> Akkadian *malkatum*) and was always written phonetically.

In contemporary Mesopotamia the king was designated by the Sumerian title lugal, translated *šarrum* in East Semitic. In Ebla, however, the lugal was a governor of the various provinces[28] while in contemporary Kish and Mari lugal designated a king.[29]

As to the meaning of the terms en, lugal and *mālikum* we have to keep in mind the warning of J.-P. Grégoire that we may too easily identify these ancient concepts with a European type of kingship. Therefore, to avoid all anachronisms and all ethnocentrisms in the explanation of these terms he forms abstracts from them: "Enate", "Lugalate" and "Malikate", respectively.[30] During the long period that we intend to cover the terms used to designate rulers had indeed different shades of meaning, but "king" and "kingship" as *we* understand it are at least functional for the present discussion.

26 Pettinato, *Ebla*, p. 109 n. 25. Fronzaroli, however, does not accept Pettinato's interpretation of nam.en = *ma-li-gú-um* = "king"; see already G. Garbini in *SEb* I/1 1979, p. 6 n. 6 and 7.

27 *Phönizisch-Punische Grammatik*. Analecta Orientalia 32, Rome 1951, § 207.

28 J.-P. Grégoire, "Remarques sur quelques noms de fonction et sur l'organisation administrative dans les archives d'Ebla", *IUO XIV*, pp. 390–392. The lugal was "governor", "superintendent", and as strategist he played a military role. Fourteen of them are known to us. The office of lugal was often exercised in Ebla by members of the family of the ruling *mālikum*.

29 Pettinato, MEE I, p. 274, and *Ebla*, pp. 73, 146.

30 *IUO XIV*, pp. 383–386.

1.3 The Concept of Kingship in Ebla

The state administration of Ebla reveals a pyramidal hierarchy with the en/*mālikum* as the supreme authority at the top of the pyramid. He was the prime administrator, chief of the army, the judge against whom there was no appeal.

1.3.1 The King as Prime Administrator

He was the head of the state and ultimately responsible for domestic and foreign policy, insofar as he guided all administrative and political functions.

High functionaries such as the Elders (ABxÁŠ = *a-bu*?)[31], governors (lugal) who directed the administrative districts[32], and the "lord" (written with the logogram M1+ŠITA :za_x = *adānu* (in Eblaic) had to report to the king. The "lord" occupied the highest rank in the administrative hierarchy, second to the king. The Eblaic equivalent *adānu* has cognates in several West-Semitic languages, e.g. Ugaritic (*adn*) and Hebrew (אדון).[33] The *nasi*$_{11}$, also to be interpreted in a West-Semitic sense (cf. Mari and the Old Testament) was a functionary of an administrative unit, especially rural.[34] Still other officials were the ugula and the *ḫazānu*.

Like all other people, the king and his family received rations but he also had to pay taxes.[35]

The king's foreign policy included supervising diplomatic marriages, contracted between royal families, and treaties that were concluded between Ebla and some neighbouring states. Probably the best known treaty was between Ebla and *Abarsal* (TM.75.G.2420), not *Ashur* as was formerly assumed. E. Sollberger, who recently studied this treaty comments: "Before turning to the translation of the treaty, it may be worth pointing out that neither the king of Ebla nor the king of Abarsal is identified. Would that be a way of indicating that the treaty is not simply between two kings but is binding in perpetuity upon the two kingdoms?"[36]

1.3.2 The King as Chief of the Army

Although the Eblaites were peaceful and built an economic-commercial rather than a political-military empire, they had to resort to arms when the need arose.

31 Grégoire, *IUO XIV*, p. 387.

32 *Ibid*, pp. 390–392. The lugal also had a military role; see Pettinato, *Akkadica* 2 (1977), pp. 23–24.

33 *Ibid*, p. 389.

34 *Ibid*, pp. 393–395.

35 Pettinato, *Ebla*, pp. 180, 189–190.

36 "The so-called treaty between Ebla and 'Ashur'", *SEb* III/9–10, p. 134. On treaties in general, including the one under discussion, see Pettinato, *Ebla*, pp. 103–105.

Mercenaries performed the work of soldiers.[37] The war between Ebla and Mari, her age-old rival, is well documented in a war bulletin (TM.75.G.2367) sent by Enna-Dagan, the Eblaite general, to the king of Ebla after he had defeated and dethroned Iblul-Il, king of Mari. "Thus Enna-Dagan, king of Mari, to the king of Ebla."[38]

An economic text (TM.G.1953) reveals that Mari had to pay tribute to the king of Ebla, perhaps as a result of this military expedition.

1.3.3 The King as Judge

The juridical texts of Ebla concern contracts of purchase and sale and the division of goods and official loans.[39] In the bilingual lists one finds the following entry: di-ku_5 = *ba-da-qù da-ne-um*, "to judge".[40]

One juridical document in the form of a letter (TM.75.G.1766) deals with a royal act according to which the king conceded as possession for a period of 10 years an agricultural property, thus immovable property, to a high functionary. The document reads: "Thus the king to Inkar, listen: for 10 years the king makes available and gives you the property in Baytayn that belongs to Tāb-Li'm, the inspector; I do not take it; for 10 years it is available and your residence shall be in the village; from time to time you shall reside in the village.
The year in which the sacrifices are brought".

P. Fronzaroli who published and studied this document, refers to similar documents of Ugarit, which were studied by G. Boyer, and in which the kings appear as protagonists. The documents, formulated in a particular manner, contain the dynastic seal and the names of witnesses.[41] Juridical documents from Hittite Hatussas (Boghazköy), the kudurru's of the Kassite period, Middle-Assyrian and Elamite laws of ± 1600 BC are also to be compared. Now the tablet, cited above, enables us to compare the juridical institutions in Syria of the third millennium with those of the second millennium BC. Though the names of neither protagonist nor that of the receiver are mentioned, and a dynastic seal as well as the names of witnesses are missing, the person of the king is in clear relief.

This document as well as others, e.g. TM.75.G.1430 and TM.75.G.1452 bear witness that juridical texts were stored in the archives of Ebla. The last

37 Pettinato, *Ebla*, pp. 99f., 119–120.

38 Pettinato, *Akkadica* 2 (1977), pp. 24ff.; *Ebla*, 99–102.

39 Pettinato, *Ebla*, p. 46.

40 *Ibid*, p. 242.

41 "La place des textes d'Ugarit dans l'histoire de l'ancien droit oriental", *Le Palais Royal d'Ugarit*. Mission de Ras Shamra, Tome VI, Paris 1955, pp. 284ff.

text, from the time of king Ebrium, explicitly states that it deals with a "decision of the king and a decision of the lord" (di-ku$_5$ en wa sa-MI+ŠITA$_x^{ki}$ di-ku$_5$).[42]

1.3.4 Eblaite Kingship and the Hereditary Principle

The texts give the impression that the king was elected for a seven-year cycle, consequently the former kings were still alive as in the time of Ebrium, a hypothesis which explains the phrase en *wa* en-en, "(for) the king and the (former) kings" in administrative texts listing rations. The hypothesis of the elected king, says Pettinato, is sustained by the ceremony of the anointing of the king, recurrent in the texts, at least in connection with the first four kings.[43] The fifth king, Ibbi-Sipiš, being the son of the fourth, ascended the throne by reason of hereditary succession. This new concept of kingship (hereditary instead of elective) explains the invention of a new calendar in the time of king Ibbi-Sipiš.[44] The dynasty of Ebla ruled for 60–70 years, and the names of five kings and their sons have been preserved.

1.3.5 King and Cult

Finally, the question is still to be answered, why en alone signified "king" in Ebla just as *maliktum* became the only indication of "queen". In Sumerian civilization the terms en and entum designated two kinds of priests.[45] The title en is one of the oldest and attested since the Uruk-epoque and designates one of the most archaic forms of the state, the "king-priest" as in Uruk. The Ebla archives emphasize the political function of this title, while in Mesopotamia the en was a high priest, whose political influence should not be underestimated, and lugal became the sole political chief. Thus the Eblaite en/*malikum* did not represent the same reality as the Mesopotamian en because they originated from two societies that differed fundamentally.[46]

The civilisation of Ebla was, according to Pettinato, essentially lay and secular despite the profound religious sense of the people. Unlike Mesopotamia where

42 P. Fronzaroli, "Un atto reale di donazione dagli Archivi di Ebla (TM.75.6.1766)". *SEb* 1/1 (1979), pp. 3–16. For TM.75.G.1452 see Pettinato MEE 1, pp. 67–68, No. 890.

43 On the ceremony of anointing see Pettinato *RBI* 25 (1977), p. 235; *Ebla*, p. 71; *BA* 43/4 (1980), pp. 205–206. A. Archi, however, differs on this point; see "The epigraphic evidence from Ebla and the Old Testament", *Biblica* 60 (1979), pp. 560–61; *BAR* Nov/Dec 1980, p. 42; "Ancora su Ebla e la Bibbia", *SEb* II/2–3, 1980, pp. 20–30.

44 Pettinato, *Ebla*, p. 146. For the old and new calendars see his "Il calendario semitico del 3. millennio recostruito sulla base dei testi di Ebla", *Or An* 16 (1977), pp. 257–285; "Il calendario di Ebla al tempo del re Ibbi-Sipiš sulla base di TM.75.G.427", *AfO* XXV (1974–1977), pp. 1–36; *Ebla*, pp. 147–153.

45 Pettinato, *Ebla*, p. 253.

46 Grégoire, *IUO* XIV, pp. 384–385.

SYRIA-PALESTINE, Amarna Age (between 1450 and 1350 BC)	ISRAEL, in the time of the monarchy, ca. 1020–587 BC
The *ḫazānu* could make decisions only as far as he was permitted by the Pharaoh.	When the authority of the head of the family was no longer unlimited, a member of a clan still had the right of appeal to the king himself (2 Sam 14:4,11). Solomon acted as judge (1 Kings 3:16 ff.).
During the Egyptian New Empire, Amurru bordered on the kingdom of Ugarit and then ʿAbdi-Aširta founded an Amorite dynasty; also elsewhere. *Bītu* "house" = dynasty. Whatever their hereditary status the succession of a Canaanite king was subject to confirmation by the Egyptian suzerain.	Saul could not establish a dynasty, as was the case with David (until 587 BC). Later, only a few kings of the Northern Kingdom succeeded in founding dynasties (Omri, Jehu). The hereditary principle was accepted.
Although Amenophis IV was more interested in religious matters than in the politics of Syria-Palestine, the El Amarna correspondence coming from local Canaanite princes provides very little information about their attitude towards the local cult.	Tendencies towards a Canaanite conception of kingship did exist, but also a reaction against it (priests). A pure secular institution did not develop: at the beginning of Israelite kingship there was the divine approval and call. In the South the charismatic call of the kings remained permanent (cf. 2 Sam 7). The end of the Israelite kingship (end 6th century BC) was rather a divine judgment than a national religious tragedy. The prophet and not the king was the mediator between God and people. Yahweh, the God of Israel, is indicated as king whose kingship would expand world-wide and cosmic, even after the Israelite kingship had disappeared.[70]

2. *Mari, Ugarit, Syria-Palestine and Israel*

MARI, late 18th century BC | UGARIT, 14th–13th century BC

1 POLITICAL SITUATION

Mari: After the assassination of king Iakhdunlim, King Shamshi-Adad I of Assyria, founder of a vast empire occupied Mari, an Amorite city-state. Zimrilim, heir to the throne, had to flee. After Shamshi-Adad's sudden death, Zimrilim regained the throne of his fathers. Mari's power was artificial, and she was ruined by king Hammurapi of Babylon.[49]

Ugarit: The kingdom of Ugarit had many natural advantages and a territory in the hinterland. Formerly within Egyptian sphere of influence, she later had, by the terms of a treaty, to recognize the Hittite king as her overlord. Sudden destruction came by the "peoples of the sea", ca. 1200 BC.[50]

2 SOURCES

Mari: Royal archives: letters and administrative texts in Akkadian of the Old Babylonian period, and include (North-)West Semitic words, phrases and personal names[53], an indication of the spoken language in the kingdom of Mari.[54]

Ugarit: Royal archives: mythological tablets in alphabetical cuneiform in which the official language, a local dialect of North Canaanite (NW Semitic), was written. Letters, legal, economic and other texts were written in Akkadian, and bilingual glossaries existed for the Hurrian-speaking minority.[55]

3 TERMS FOR "KING" AND "KINGSHIP"

Mari: Various terms are used:[58]

1) a d . d a kur Mar.tu (*abu Amurrim*), "father of the Amorites", "Father" as an overlord in treaties.
2) *šarru* (l u g a l), "king", *šarrûtum*, "kingship", cf. Hebrew שַׂר. Nomadic Yaminites knew a hierarchy with *šarranu(meš)* at the top. Palestinian rulers of Mari Age known as *šarru*. An overlord = *šarru rabû*, "great king". *šarrūtum epēšum* = "to exercise kingship".
3) *Mālikū* (plural), *maliku(m)* or *malku(m)* (singular) = "ruler", "king"; *mālikum*, "counsellor". *Malik*, *milk-* in personal names (Huffmon, pp. 230–31). *Namlākātum*, "kingdom"; cf. Hebrew מַמְלָכוֹת (pl.)
4) *Nasi* in the name of a divinity. Cf. Ebla (p. 6 above) and the OT: "chief, leader".
5) *Awīlum*, "free man", "king".
6) ^{lu} *ša-pi-tum*, √ *špṭ*, "exercise authority, judge". Cf. Hebrew שֹׁפֵט "judge".

Ugarit:

1) *šarru* (l u g a l)
2) *mlk*[59]. The root *mlk* in personal names:
   -malak
   -^{d}*mālik*
   milki-
   -milki/n
   -mlk-
   -mlk
   Name of a deity, Akkadian ^{d}*malik*, West-Semitic *muluk*[60]
3) e n = *bēlu* for the governor of Ugarit.[61]

4 THE CONCEPT OF KINGSHIP

4.1 The king as prime administrator

Mari: The palace administration controlled the economy firmly (see *ARMT IX*). The king was responsible for the agriculture and harvests and he remained the final landowner (cf. Ugarit), thus he prevented an uncontrolled influx of nomads, such as the Hanaeans. The "anointment (?) of the king" seems to have been a daily ritual.

Ugarit: The king was the supreme authority in civil affairs.

4.2 The king as commander of the army

Mari: During the reign of Zimrilim he had to wage many wars and the army was under his direct control.

Ugarit: According to the ideal kingship of ancient Canaan (c. 1800 BC) Krt personally led a military expedition. Under Hittite supremacy the Ugaritic king was still supreme authority in military affairs, but no more under his personal leadership.

SYRIA-PALESTINE, Amarna Age (between 1450 and 1350 BC)

During the two centuries of Egyptian occupation (18th and 19th dynasty) of Southern Syria and Palestine (16th century BC) their political organization became quite normalized. The Egyptians left the local princely houses in control of their own territories, but under close supervision of Egyptian agents. Disinterest of the pharaohs and exploitation led to a deterioration of Egyptian and Canaanite morale.[51] Egyptian Syria-Palestine was divided into 3 provinces. (W. Helck).

The tablets are mostly letters from the royal archives of Amenophis IV or Akhenaten (1379–1362 BC) and his father, Amenophis III (1417–1379 BC). The Akkadian of the letters reveal Old Babylonian archaisms, similar to the language used by Amorite scribes in the 18th and 17th centuries in Syria and Upper Mesopotamia. They also abound with Canaanitisms.[56]

1) *amīlu*, "free man", "chief" (of GN) the official title.
2) *ḫāzianu* (*ḫazānu*), "governor" their office
3) In Canaanite circles "king", Akkadian *šarru* Canaanite *milku*[62], *maliku*/*malku*, "ruler, adviser"[63], in theophoric names Abimilki and Milkilu[64]
4) en = *bēlu* for the city-king (of Ammia and Byblos). In the king the people of a territory are identified as a group. He is their "lord" and they are his "slaves".[65]

Egypt continued the Hyksos feudal system of city-states, each with its own dynasty. Each of these petty kings could govern his subjects as long as he supplied tribute and corvée. A double system of administration existed: a) local, feudal princes (*ḫazianu*, *ḫazānu* = governor); b) Egyptian commissaries (*rābiṣu* appointed by the Pharaoh. Here Canaanite kingship, contrary to that in Ugarit, was degenerated to a mere governorship.

There were Egyptian troops in Syria and Palestine. Egypt also used the local aristocracy, the *maryannu* from whom they recruited the *ḫazānūtu* to subdue the indigenous people. The *ḫazānūtu* had their own soldiers.

ISRAEL, in the time of the monarchy, ca 1020–587 BC

In the latter part of the 11th century BC the Philistine crisis brought the Israelite tribal league to an end. While in this situation Israel elected Saul to be her first king. The step was taken by some with great reluctance, for a monarchy was an institution totally foreign to Israel's tradition.[52] The united monarchy of Israel was established (David, Solomon), later divided into the kingdoms of Israel and Juda, and came to an end in 722 and 586 BC respectively.

The concept of "king" is found in all the books of the Hebrew Old Testament, thus in a variety of literary genres.[57] It is, however, in the historical and prophetic books that the conception of kingship in Israel is described. Hebrew, "the language of Canaan" (Is 19:18) is cognate to Eblaic (Old-Canaanite), the Amorite of Mari, Ugaritic and the Canaanite of the Amarna Age.

1) נָגִיד "chief, leader"
2) מֶלֶךְ
Saul is not referred to as a king (מֶלֶךְ) but as a "leader" or "commander" (נָגִיד). Samuel and the tribal elders probably never intended to elevate Saul to kingship in the conventional sense at all, but merely wished him to serve as the elected military leader of the tribes on a permanent basis. The people, however, thought of Saul as a king and addressed him as such (J. Bright, *A History of Israel*, p. 190).

Little is known about the administration of the kingdom under David. From the time of Solomon, however, we have a list of 12 prefects with the description of the lands they governed (1 Kings 4:7–19; cf. the Ugaritic administrative lists). They collected taxes. The king remained the prime administrator.

Throughout the history of the monarchy it is clear that the king was the real commander of the army and leader in war.

4.3 The king as judge

The king was entitled *lušāpitum*, and he acted as the highest appeal. 103 legal texts from Mari are published and discussed by G. Boyer (*ARM VIII*), and we may assume that he acted as judge according to these legal principles. An ordeal could be decisive (River god).

Unlike Mesopotamia juridical texts from Syria and Palestine were extremely rare until the discoveries at Ugarit and Alalaḫ. Their principal characteristic is the special place assigned to the king, acting as representative of public authority: judgment is represented as his personal act without reference to a law of the state.[66] Krt had to judge the case of the widow and the oppressed.[67]

4.4 The hereditary principle and kingship

The so-called Lim-dynasty in Mari, founded by Yaggid-Lim (Lim: a great god of the Amorites) probably originated from the nomadic Ḫanaeans.

A hereditary dynasty was founded in Ugarit that was maintained under Hittite suzerainty. An old dynastic seal on contracts was used.

4.5 King and cult

A large mural painting depicted the ceremony by which Zimrilim was inaugurated as king in front of the goddess Ištar from whom he received a staff and a ring as the symbols of the authority of the goddess. Divination was important and the king wrote a letter to the River god. Prophets revealed the god's will to the king. The "national" god Dagān helped Zimrilim to conquer the nomadic Yaminites. The ban (*asakkam akālum*, "to eat the *asakku*", i.e. something forbidden, tabu for god or king), was used in an oath formula.

A list of deified kings of Ugarit, dated to the beginning of the 2nd millennium BC, is discovered, and was used as a cult.[68] The list ends with *'il nqmd, 'il yqr*, known as kings of the dynastic seal. The conception was that El was the father of Krt (*UT* Krt, 40–41). Thus Krt was the representative of his sacral community and the executive of the god's order in society. The king was also "servant" (*'bd*) of El, set aside by the rite of anointing, became a priest, and performed sacrifice. Ideal kingship was like this in the heroic age, but the situation changed for reigning kings at the end of LB.[69]

the clergy and the temple played key roles in political and economic affairs, the Ebla texts suggest a sharp distinction between political and religious spheres.[47]

Furthermore, if we accept the viewpoint of Pettinato and Gelb that Eblaic was used much more than Sumerian, then en was a mere logogram for the West-Semitic concept *mālikum* that differed from what en originally meant and still meant in contemporary Mesopotamia.

Pettinato's conclusion that the Ebla of the third millennium BC was essentially a secular state is a remarkable confirmation of Frankfort's analysis of kingship in the ancient Near East, outside Egypt and Mesopotamia. A secular state, however, was still difficult to visualize because the sense of the religious in the ancient Near East was exceptionally strong. This is well demonstrated by the role of the king and his family when they offered sacrifices as part of the official cult in Ebla.[48]

Conclusions

1 *Mlk* is a common Semitic root but only in the North-west (now also Ebla) and South-Semitic languages does it have the meaning "to be king". *Mèlèk* (and equivalents), "king" was used for all kinds of monarchical rulers (city-states, lands, territories, tribes).

2 In the whole Semitic world divinities were entitled as king.

3 Unlike Egypt and Mesopotamia where the deified and human kings respectively acted as mediator between the gods and the people, kingship was more secularized amongst the NW-Semitic peoples in Syria and Palestine, but then not as radical as we may deduce from Frankfort's book. The king had to take care of his people in all walks of life (administration, defence, jurisprudence, cult).

4 While the king had to keep in equilibrium the all important relation between nature and people of the ancient near East, and for whom the fertility rituals were a necessity, nature was completely demythologized and secularized in Israel. Thus a new dimension was added to the kingship of God, and man could truly have dominion over nature (cf. Gen 1:28).

47 Pettinato, *Ebla*, pp. 244–45; cf. Grégoire, *IUO* XIV, pp. 397–98.

48 Cf. Pettinato, "Culto ufficiale ad Ebla durante il regno di Ibbi-Sipiš", *Or An* 18 (1979), pp. 96–101.

49 For the history of Syria in the second millennium BC see H. Klengel, *Geschichte Syriens im 2. Jahrtausend v u Z* I 1965; II 1969; III 1970, Berlin. For Mari see F. M. Tocci, *La Siria nell' età di Mari.* Studi Semitici 3, Rome 1960; J.-R. Kupper, *Northern Mesopotamia and Syria*. The Cambridge Ancient History, revised edition (= CAH), vol. II, Ch. I, Cambridge 1963.

50 M. Liverani, *Storia di Ugarit nell' età degli archivi politici*. Studi Semitici 6, Rome 1962; M. S. Drower, *Ugarit*. CAH, vol. II, ch. XXI (b), Cambridge 1968.

51 W. F. Albright, *The Amarna Letters from Palestine*. CAH, vol. II. ch. XX, Cambridge 1966.

52 See I. Mendelsohn, "Samuel's denunciation of kingship in the light of the Akkadian documents from Ugarit", *BASOR* 143 (1956), pp. 17–22.

53 H. B. Huffmon, *Amorite personal names in the Mari Texts*, Baltimore 1965.

54 Mari text publications appear in the series *Archives royales de Mari*, 1946–, and in a wide variety of publications. See Huffmon, *op. cit.*, pp. 274–77.

55 Ugaritic text publications: *Palais royal d'Ugarit* II 1957; III 1955; IV 1956; V 1965; VI 1970. A. Herdner, *Corpus des textes en cunéiformes alphabétiques de Ras Shamra, Campagnes I à XI, 1929 à 1939*, Paris 1963; C. H. Gordon, *Ugaritic Manual,* Rome 1955; M. Dietrich–O. Loretz – J. Sanmartín, *Die keilalphabetischen Texte aus Ugarit.* Alter Orient und Altes Testament 24, Kevelaer 1976.

56 Albright, *op. cit.* (n. 51 above), p. 4. The El-Amarna Letters were published by J. A. Knudtson – O. Weber – E. Ebeling, *Die El-Amarna Tafeln*, Vorderasiatische Bibliothek 2, Leipzig 1907–1915. Reprint Aalen 1964; A. F. Rainey, *El Amarna Tablets* 359–379, Alter Orient und Altes Testament 8, Kevelaer 1970.

57 J. A. Soggin, מלך , in *Theologisches Handwörterbuch zum Alten Testament*, editors E. Jenni – C. Westermann, München–Zürich, Vol. II, 1976, col. 909.

58 L. M. Muntingh, "Israelite-Amorite political relations during the second millennium BC in the light of Near Eastern politics. A study of relevant Amorite, Akkadian and Hebrew concepts", *Atti del secondo congresso internazionale di linguistica Camito-Semitica,* Florence 16–19 April 1974 (ed. P. Fronzaroli), Florence 1978, pp. 217–221.

59 PRU II, p. 211.

60 F. Grøndahl, *Die Personennamen der Texte aus Ugarit*, Rome 1967, pp. 157–58.

61 G. Buccellati, *Cities and Nations of Ancient Syria*. Studi Semitici 26, Rome 1967, p. 50.

62 W. F. Albright, *op. cit.* (n. 51), p. 8.

63 J. A. Knudtzon, *op. cit.*, p. 1462.

64 J. Gray, *The Canaanites*. Ancient peoples and places. London 1965, p. 125.

65 Buccellati, *op. cit.* (n. 61 above), pp. 59–60.

66 R. de Vaux, *Ancient Israel. Its life and Institutions*. London 1961, p. 146. For the juridical texts of Ugarit, studied by G. Boyer, see p. 7 above.

67 J. Gray, *The Canaanites*, pp. 108–109.

68 RS 24.257, *Ugaritica* V, pp. 561–62, No. 5; *KTU* 119, No. 1.113; cf. K. A. Kitchen, "The King List of Ugarit", *UF* 9 (1977), pp. 131–42.

69 J. Gray, "Sacral kingship in Ugarit", *Ugaritica* VI, 1969, pp. 289–302.

70 J. A. Soggin, *THAT*, col. 908–919 (see n. 57).

David Toshio Tsumura (University of Tsukuba)

THE PROBLEM OF CHILDLESSNESS IN THE ROYAL EPIC OF UGARIT*

An Analysis of KRT[KTU 1.14:I]:1–25

In any monarchical society, the "childlessness" of the ruling king is a crucial problem; it would mean the discontinuance of his dynasty, which subsequently would cause disorder or instability in the society. For this reason, the "royal succession" for the survival of the dynasty is the basic concern of the ancient monarchs, and "childlessness" is the fundamental problem in the royal epics[1] of the ancient world.

In general, "childlessness" is caused by one of the following:[2]

(1) sterility, i.e. barrenness of one of the spouses
(2) widowhood without a child, i.e. the death of a spouse before a child is born, or more accurately, conceived
(3) loss of children in old age, i.e. after one or both of the spouses becomes barren
(4) loss of children in widowhood.

For this problem of "childlessness", various solutions were proposed in the customs of the ancient Near East: e.g. (a) adoption, (b) taking another woman, either as a "second" wife or as a substitute for the first one, (c) levirate marriage,

* Abbreviations in this paper follow that of *Ugarit Forschungen* 11 (1979).

1 See recent discussion on this topic in Stan Rummel, "Narrative Structures in the Ugaritic Texts", in S. Rummel (ed.), *RSP* 3 (1981), pp. 221–332, especially pp. 328–331.

2 The following are examples for each category:
(1) the initial state of childlessness of Abram (Abraham) in Genesis story, of Zacharia in Luke's Gospel story, and of many others, because of their spouse' sterility; also the case of the king Daniel of the Aqhat Epic (see below) and Etana in an Akkadian story;
(2) Ruth's situation before her marriage with Boaz;
(3) the possible "death of child in old age" in the case of the test of Abraham's faith in Genesis 22 where his God asks him to sacrifice his only legitimate successor, Isaac;
(4) Naomi's loss of her sons after her husband passed away and a widow's loss of her only son in Luke 7.

etc.[3] In the royal epics, however, the solution often comes from the direct intervention of a deity who "blesses" a son to the king.

In the two Ugaritic epics, Krt and Aqht, the common topic is that a king without an heir has male offspring by the blessing of the god El. Both kings, Keret and Daniel, who are deeply concerned with their "childlessness", resort to incubation to obtain a divine promise of offspring.[4] However, the cause of the initial state of childlessness is different. In the Aqht Epic, the king Daniel was childless because of sterility (case 1).[5] On the other hand in the Krt Epic, the king's childless state was brought about by a different cause.

The nature of this cause is highly disputed: there are two major explanations.

[A] Keret has no heir because of the death of all his children after his legitimate wife "departed", i.e. the loss of a wife and subsequent death of all his sons (case 4).[6]

[B] Keret has no heir because of the death of his seven wives one after another before he could have children by them, i.e. the loss of all the wives before a son could be born (case 2).[7]

3 See the following articles: Tikva Frymer-Kensky, "Patriarchal Family Relationships and Near Eastern Law"; *BA* 44 (1981), pp. 209–214; John van Seters, "The Problem of Childlessness in Near Eastern Law and the Patriarchs of Israel," *JBL* 87 (1968), pp. 401–408; Samson Kardimon, "Adoption as a Remedy for Infertility in the Period of the Patriarchs," *JSS* 3 (1958), pp. 123–126; Millar Burrows, "The Ancient Oriental Background of Hebrew Levirate Marriage," *BASOR* 77 (1940), pp. 2–15; Raymond Westbrook, "The Law of the Biblical Levirate," *Revue Internationale des Droits de l'antiquité* 3ᵉ série 24 (1977), pp. 65–87.

4 Cf. Cyrus H. Gordon, *The Common Background of Greek and Hebrew Civilizations* (New York, 1962, 1965), p. 156.

5 Note that Daniel's wife is still alive and yet "he has no son like his brothers" (KTU 1.17/UT 2 Aqht I:18–19).

6 E.g., H. L. Ginsberg, *LKK* (1946), pp. 14 & 33; C. H. Gordon, *UL* (1949), p. 67 & *PLMU* [= "Poetic Legends and Myths from Ugarit," *Berytus* 25 (1977), pp. 5–133], p. 37; G. R. Driver, *CML* (1956), p. 29 & "Ugaritic Problems," in S. Segert (ed.), *Studia Semitica: Ioanni Bakoš Dedicata* (Bratislava, 1965), pp. 95f.; J. Gray, *LC*^{2} (1965), pp. 132ff. & *KRT*^{2} [= *The Krt Text in the Literature of Ras Shamra* (Leiden, 1964)], pp. 11 & 32f.; F. C. Fensham, "Remarks on Certain Difficult Passages in Keret," *JNSL* 1 (1971), pp. 18–21; M. Dietrich – O. Loretz, "Der Prolog des Krt-Epos (CTA 14 I 1–35)," in H. Gese & H. P. Rüger (eds.), *Wort und Geschichte: Festschrift für Karl Elliger zum 70. Geburtstag* (*AOAT* 18) (Neukirchen-Vluyn, 1973), pp. 32–34, & "Das Porträt einer Königin in KTU 1.14 I 12–15," *UF* 12 (1980), pp. 202–4; A. Caquot *et al, TO* (1974), pp. 505f.; M. D. Coogan, *Stories from Ancient Canaan* (Philadelphia, 1978), p. 58; D. Kinet, *Ugarit: Geschichte und Kultur einer Stadt in der Umwelt des Alten Testamentes* (Stuttgart, 1981), pp. 112f.

7 E.g., U. Cassuto, "The Seven Wives of King Keret," *BASOR* 119 (1950), pp. 18–20; A. van Selms, *MFUL* (1954), p. 97, & "The Root *k-ṯ-r* and its Derivatives in Ugaritic Literature," *UF* 11 (1979), p. 742; J. Aistleitner, *MKT*^{2} [= *Die Mythologischen und Kultischen Texte aus Ras Schamra* (Budapest, 1964)], pp. 87ff.; H. Sauren – G. Kestemont, "Keret, roi de Ḫubur," *UF* 3 (1971), pp.

The difference in these positions is based not only on the philological interpretation of particular words such as *ṯar um* and *mqtlt*-form numerals, but also on the understanding of the nature of childlessness and the literary structure and motif of this epic.

KRT[KTU 1.14:I]:1–25

(1) [lk]rt	Of Krt
(2) [ ] .mlk[ ]	. . . . . . king . . . .
(3) [ ]m.k[ ]	. . . .
(4) [ ]	. . . .
(5) [ ]m.il [ ]	. . . . El . . . .
(6) [ ]dnhr.	. . . . river.
umt /[krt.]^{c}(?)rwt.[8]	*The clan of Krt* was destroyed[9]
bt /[m]lk.itb!d!(itdb).	*the house of the king* was perished.
dšb^{c} /[a]ḫm.lh	It had seven brothers[10]
ṯmnt.bn um	eight sons of a mother.
(10) krt.ḥtkn.rš	{ Krt, *his offspring*[11] was ruined
(11) krt.grdš.mknt	{ Krt, *(his) dynasty* was finished![12]

194f.; B. Margalit, "Studia Ugaritica II: Studies in *Krt* and *Aqht*," *UF* 8 (1976), pp. 137–145; J. C. L. Gibson, *CML*^{2} (1978), pp. 20 & 82; J. C. de Moor, "Contributions to the Ugaritic Lexicon," *UF* 11 (1979), pp. 643f.; P. C. Craigie, *Ugarit and the Old Testament* (Grand Rapids, 1983), p. 56.

8 For this reading, see *KTU*, p. 38. Cf. Dietrich – Loretz in *AOAT* 18, p. 33; J. C. de Moor – K. Spronk, "Problematical Passages in the Legend of Kirtu (I)," *UF* 14 (1982), p. 154.

9 Cf. Dietrich – Loretz in *AOAT* 18, p. 32: "Die Sippe Krt's ist vernichtet"; L. Badre *et al*, "Notes Ougaritiques I: Keret," *Syria* 53 (1976), p. 96. De Moor – Spronk, *UF* 14, p. 154 is probably right in taking *rš* // *grdš* (ll. 10–11) as balancing the parallelism of *^{c}rwt* // *itbd*, since the subjects of these "predicates" also correspond to each other in meaning: "offspring" // "dynasty" (which is in variant with "royal house" in l. 23) and "clan" // "house".

10 On *aḫ* "male offspring", see below.

11 The term *ḥtk* would mean either "father" or "son": see C. H. Gordon, *UT* 19.911; Dennis Pardee, "The New Canaanite Myths and Legends," *BO* 37 (1980), pp. 284f. & others. Note also the recent proposal to take *ḥtk* as "authority": de Moor – Spronk, *UF* 14, p. 154; Dietrich – Loretz in *AOAT* 18, p. 33; Fensham, *JNSL* 1, p. 16. However, when the preceeding context is taken to describe Keret's seven "sons", as discussed below, there is no necessity to distinguish *ḥtk* (l. 10) and *ḥtk* (ll. 21–22) by translating them "government" and "offspring" (Fensham), or "patriarch" and "offspring" (Coogan, *Stories*, p. 58). The context seems to support more ordinary sense, "son", "offspring" or the like, for *ḥtk* in all three places. For the suffix *n*, see Pardee, *BO* 37, p. 284; Badre *et al*, *Syria* 53, p. 97; de Moor – Spronk, *UF* 14, p. 154.

12 For a recent view to take *grdš* as a noun phrase which might mean "a ruin" (from a root *gdš), see de Moor – Spronk, *UF* 14, p. 155.

(12) aṯt.ṣdqh.lypq	(i) *His legitimate wife*[13] he did not keep
(13) mtrḫt.yšrh	his lawful spouse
(14) aṯt.trḫ.wtb^{c}t	the wife he married indeed departed.[14]
(15) ṯar um.tkn lh	(ii) *Progeny of (one) mother* had been his.
(16) mṯlṯt. kṯrm.tmt	One third died at birth
(17) mrb^{c}t.zblnm	one fourth, of disease.
(18) mḫmšt.yitsp /ršp[.]	One fifth Rašpu gathered in
mṯdṯt.ġlm /ym.	one sixth, the Lads of Yamm.
mšb^{c}t hn.bšlḥ /ttpl.	One seventh, lo! by the sword they fell.[15]
y^{c}n.ḥtkh /krt.	{ Krt sees *his offspring*
y^{c}n.ḥtkh rš	{ he sees *his offspring* ruined
(23) mid.grdš.ṯbth	{ *his royal house* completely finished.

13 For the "legitimate wife" (*aṯt.ṣdq*) //"lawful spouse" (*mtrḫt. yšr*), cf. *aššāt šīmātim* "the lawful spouses" (Gilg. P. iv 32) which A. Heidel explains as "(cum) uxoribus destinatis" in his *The Gilgamesh Epic and Old Testament Parallels* (Chicago, 1949), p. 30. See *CAD* (A/2), p. 465, and also below.

14 In their most recent analysis of lines 12–14, Dietrich – Loretz [*UF* 12, pp. 200f.; cf. *AOAT* 18, p. 32 & "Der Prolog des Krt-Epos," *UF* 5 (1973), p. 283] take them as a tricolon, where three sets of parallel terms are recognized: *aṯt //mtrḫt // aṯt, ṣdg //yšr* & **pwq //trḫ*. However, the last pair might well be *l-ypq //w-tb^{c}t* which seem to be synonymous verbal phrases: "did not keep" //"indeed departed". For the similar semantic range, "to get" ~ "to keep", see *qanû* "to buy, acquire" & "to keep" in Akkadian. Cf. *CAD* (Q), p. 91. De Moor – Spronk's denial of Dietrich – Loretz' above analysis (cf. *UF* 14, p. 155, n. 20) cannot be supported for the following reasons: (1) there is no reason why we should not find here a tricolon, even from the viewpoint of the "principle of *external* parallelism". Whether "all the preceding and following verses" of lines 12–13 are bicola is not settled, for lines 21b–23 certainly constitute a three-line "expanded colon". Moreover, to find a unicolon, or "monocolon" in S. Segert's terminology [cf. "Parallelism in Ugaritic Poetry", *JAOS* 103 (1983), p. 297], in an isolated place (i.e. l. 15) is not an unwelcomed matter; this line is structurally in balance with lines 20b–21a which also constitutes a monocolon with a climactic effect: *mšb^{c}t hn.bšlḥ /ttpl* [see below]. There seems therefore to exist in this section of the text the following symmetrical pattern:

10–11	: bicolon		
12–14	:	tricolon	
15	:		monocolon
16–17	: bicolon		
18–20a	: bicolon		
20b–21a	:		monocolon
21b–23	:	tricolon	
24–25	: bicolon		

(2) the scribal practice of dividing lines should not be a strong factor in considering the matter of stichometry. The very fact that the line-division and the stichometry do not agree in ll. 6–9 as well as in ll. 18–22 illustrates the counter argument.

15 Following Gordons's translation in *PLMU*, p. 37 with minor changes.

(24) wbtmhn.[16]špḥ.yitbd — Indeed in its totality *the family* was perished

(25) wb.pḫyrh.yrṯ — indeed in his entirety, *(every) heir.*

Without going into a detailed philological discussion of those difficult words, I would like to make several observations:

1. Those who take [B] position disagree with each other on how to read the text in line 15. According to my research, five different emendations have been suggested:[17] i.e. *ṯtr um* (Aistleitner), *ṯnt um* (Sauren & Kestemont), *ṯnt.um* (Gibson), ⟨*a/m*⟩*ṯt*[.]*rumt* (Margalit) and *ṯar um* ⟨*l*⟩*tkn* (de Moor).

2. Among those who take [B] position, Cassuto and de Moor agree in taking *aṯt.ṣdqh* (l. 12) as referring to the first wife and *aṯt.trḫ* (1.14) as referring to the second.[18] Others, except Aistleitner, take *aṯt.trḫ* (1.14) as referring to the first wife and the emended text, *ṯnt um* or ⟨*a/m*⟩*ṯt*, in line 15 as referring to the second one.[19] However, in this case, ll. 12–13 seems to be out of place, without any adequate explanation of the meaning and function of *aṯt.ṣdqh // mtrḫt. yšrh* whom he "did not get/find."[20]

3. Those who take [B] position are obliged to oppose the "fraction" interpretation of *mqtlt*-form numerals.[21] However, since the sum of $\frac{1}{3}+\frac{1}{4}+\frac{1}{5}+\frac{1}{6}+\frac{1}{7}$ is $\frac{153}{140} \doteqdot 1.09$, which is slightly more than 1, "the approximation is good enough, at least literarily, to signify totality."[22] De Moor recently opposed the fraction-theory just because the numerals begin with $\frac{1}{3}$, or a numeral related to 3, without the numerals related to 1 and 2.[23] But there seems to be a mathematical reason for this. Namely, if the numeral series started with $\frac{1}{2}$, then $\frac{1}{2}+\ldots\ldots+\frac{1}{7}=\frac{223}{140}=1.59$

16 See de Moor – Spronk, *UF* 14, p. 156, who are in favor of *CTA* reading, against *KTU*'s: *wbklhn*.

17 Aistleitner, *MKT*², p. 89; Sauren – Kestemont, *UF* 3, p. 194; Gibson, *CML*², p. 82; Margalit, *UF* 8, pp. 140f.; de Moor, *UF* 11, p. 644.

18 Cassuto, *BASOR* 119, p. 19; de Moor, *UF* 11, p. 644. Cf. Badre *et al, Syria* 53, p. 97 who also take *aṯt* (l. 12) and *aṯt* (l. 14) as the first and second wives, though they take *mṯlṯt* and other forms as referring to "the children born of the third wife", etc., thus taking non [B] position.

19 I.e., Sauren – Kestemont, Margalit, Gibson & others.

20 See Pardee's criticism of Gibson; *CML*² on this matter in *BO* 37, p. 285.

21 It seems that the change of Driver's position from the "accepted interpretation of the text" in *CML*, p. 29 to the nonfractionist interpretation in *Studia Semitica*, p. 95 was possibly due to his belief that the sum of $\frac{1}{3}+\frac{1}{4}+\frac{1}{5}+\frac{1}{6}+\frac{1}{7}$ was $\frac{459}{520}$, instead of the accurate $\frac{459}{420}=\frac{153}{140}$. Note a new example of *mqtlt*-form numeral in RS 24.229, l. 3: *mṯlṯt* (*Ug* VII, p. 68f.); *KTU*'s reading, *mṯlṯ* (KTU 1.98:3), is wrong, if the A. Herdner's hand-copy text is correct. For other examples, see Gordon, *UT*, pp. 50, 403, 482 & 556.

22 Gordon, *PLMU*, p. 37, no. 38.

23 De Moor, *UF* 11, p. 643: "any interpretation taking the *mqtlt*-forms as designations of the children is complicated by the circumstance that the series does not start with '1–2' or '½', as one would expect, but with '3' or '⅓.'"

would be too large to signify "totality"; on the other hand, if it started with $\frac{1}{4}$, then the total is $\frac{319}{420}$= 0.76 which would be too small for 1.[24]

Because of philological difficulties in this section of the Epic there has been no systematic handling of literary phenomena so far. Here I would like to present a more overall analysis of the literary structure.

[I] *Repetition / Correspondence*

Our first observation in terms of literary phenomena is the repetition of word, phrase and parallelism. It is almost certain that the root 'bd is involved in the spelling of *itdb* in l. 8, which corresponds to *yitbd* in l. 24. And *ḥtk* (l. 10) "offspring" is repeated in ll. 21 and 22. The word pair *rš* // *grdš* (l. 10–11) appears also in ll. 22–23. Moreover, *mknt* (l. 11) and *ṯbt* (l. 23) are so-called synonymous variants[25], both signifying "royal house".

The two-line parallelism in ll. 10–11 is thus expanded, with variation, to a three-line "expanded colon"[26] in ll. 21–23. In this way, the "destruction" (*rš* // *grdš*) of the "royal house" (*ṯbt*) and "offspring" (*ḥtk*) is described emphatically in the repeated parallelism.

It is important to note here that *bt* [*m*]*lk* (ll. 7–8) does not simply mean a building.[27] *Bt* in the present context means "household, family, royal house"[28] like the Akkadian *bītu* and the Hebrew *byt* as well as Japanese "ie". Hence, destruction of the royal house would mean the extinction of the dynasty without an heir. For the monarch who is deeply concerned with his succession, "childlessness" *is* the destruction of his dynasty (*bt mlk*), even though he might have much gold and silver.[29] Therefore, it is not surprising in this literary framework that the

24 See Joshua Finkel, "A Mathematical Conundrum in the Ugaritic Keret Poem," *HUCA* 26 (1955), pp. 109–149 for different explanations about this mathematical matter.

25 Cf. S. Talmon, "Synonymous Readings in the Textual Traditions of the Old Testament," *Scripta Hierosolymitana* 8 (1961), pp. 335–383.

26 Cf. S. E. Loewenstamm, "The Expanded Colon in Ugaritic and Biblical Verse," *JSS* 14 (1969), pp. 176–196; "The Expanded Colon, Reconsidered," *UF* 7 (1975), pp. 261–264; etc.

27 Note Gibson's comment: "The destruction (or restoration) of Keret's palace is not a motif in the story," in *CML*², p. 82, no. 1. Cf. Driver, *CML*, pp. 2 & 5; Gray, *KRT*², p. 31; S. Rummel, in *RSP* 3, p. 303, no. 10, who all take this *bt* as a "palace".

28 *CAD* (B), pp. 293ff.

29 See KTU 1.14:III:33–34, 38 /UT Krt: 137–138, 142: "What need have I for silver / And yellow gold together with its place . . .? But what is not in my house shalt thou give!" (Gordon, *PLMU*, p. 42). In this point, the Epic of Keret is fundamentally different from the Book of Job in their motif (against Coogan, *Stories*, p. 52: "Kirta's situation recalls that of Job, a comparison strengthened

destruction (*'bd*) of "family" (*šph̩*) // "heir" (*yrṯ*) in ll. 24–25 corresponds to the destruction (*ʿrw* // *'bd*) of the "royal house" (*bt mlk*) in ll. 7–8.

Numerals in this initial section of the Epic seem to correspond to each other; "seven" (*šbʿ*) // "eight" (*ṯmn*) in ll. 8–9 and the series of fractions, $\frac{1}{3}+\frac{1}{4}+\frac{1}{5}+\frac{1}{6}+\frac{1}{7}$, are significantly related, both having the root **šbʿ* in their literary expressions, especially when both are taken as the numbers of Keret's sons.

Now, the expression *šbʿ* [*a*]*ḫm* //*ṯmnt.bn um* in ll. 8–9 has been understood as meaning either Keret's "seven brothers" or his "seven sons". Gordon, Driver, recently Coogan and others[30] take [*m*]*lk* as the antecedent of the relative pronoun *d* in line 8, thus taking the above expression as meaning Keret's "seven brothers". On the other hand, Ginsberg, Gray, Gibson *et al*[31] take *bt* [*m*]lk (ll. 7–8) as its antecedent. Grammatically, both positions are possible. In the latter position, the expression, *dšbʿ* [*a*]*ḫm.lh* (ll. 8–9), means that the royal house had seven "brothers". Now since the term *aḫ* can mean, as in Hebrew, "any male member of the *mišpāḥāh*" as well as "brother"[32], the expression "seven brothers" does not necessarily mean "seven brothers" of the king himself. Hence, *šbʿ* [*a*]*ḫm* could signify "seven male offspring" of the royal house (*bt mlk*). In fact Gray takes this *aḫm* // *bn um* as "Krt's sons by one wife."[33] I would take them as Keret's seven sons by his "legitimate wife" (*aṯt.ṣdqh*), just like seven children promised to Keret through his destined wife Ḥry later in the Epic.[34] Thus, in this very beginning portion of the epic, there is mention of the initial "perfect" state with an ideal number of sons,[35] who will

by Kirta's sickness described in the second and third tablets" and M. H. Lichtenstein, *Episodic Structure in the Ugaritic Keret Legend* (Ann Arbor, 1979), pp. 423ff.).

30 Gordon, *UL*, p. 67; *PLMU*, p. 37; Driver, *CML*, p. 29; Coogan, *Stories*, p. 58; Cassuto, BASOR 119, p. 18; Dietrich-Loretz in *AOAT* 18, p. 32; Badre *et al*, *Syria* 53, p. 97 & others.

31 Ginsberg, *LKK*, p. 14; Gray, *KRT*², p. 30; Gibson, *CML*², p. 82; Aistleitner, *MKT*², p. 88; Caquot *et al*, *TO*, p. 503 & others.

32 Francis I. Andersen, "Israelite Kinship Terminology and Social Structure," *The Bible Translator* 20 (1969), p. 38.

33 Gray, *KRT*², p. 30.

34 KTU 1.15 / UT 128:II:23 reads: "(Ḥry) will bear thee seven sons" (*tld.šbʿ bnm lk*). However, this *šbʿ bnm* could be in the sense of "seven offsprings" which includes both male and female children of Keret. In fact, Keret had only two named sons, i.e. Yṣb and Ilḥu and KTU 1.15 /UT 128:III:21 (*wtqrb.wld.bnm lh*) would probably mean: "And she comes to term to bear him (two) sons". Cf. Gordon, *PLMU*, p. 48; Gray, *KRT*², p. 19; Caquot *et al*, *TO*, p. 541, no. q. If the sixfold repetition of *tld.pġt* in KTU 1.15 / UT 128:III:7–12 signifies the birth of Keret's daughters, the actual number of Keret's "offspring" by Ḥry would be two sons & six daughters, the eighth one being a daughter Ṯtmnt (cf. KTU 1.15 / UT 128:II:24). Note the number parallelism, "seven" // "eight", both in KTU 1.14 / UT Krt:8–9 and KTU 1.15 / UT 128:II:23–24.

35 For the motif of "a mother of seven children", see D. T. Tsumura, *The Ugaritic Drama of the Good Gods* (Ann Arbor, 1973), pp. 192–194.

subsequently be lost "completely",[36] after the loss of their mother who was Keret's legitimate wife.

[II] *General-Detailed Pattern*[37]

In the light of the above observations, I would like to analyze the overall structure of the initial section as follows: the ⟨general outline⟩ of the destruction of the "royal house" (*bt mlk*) is given in ll. 1–11; then a ⟨detailed description⟩ of the destruction of the royal house as the result of loss of wife (*at̲t̲*) and sons is provided in ll. 12–25.[38] This framework seems to be supported by the existence of the two-line parallelism (ll. 10–11) in the earlier section and the three-line "expanded" colon (ll. 21–23) in the latter section, just as the Aqht epic uses a similar technique of utilizing the "expanded colon" for the ⟨detailed description⟩.[39]

36 Note that the "complete" death of the "perfect" number of sons in this text could be explained mathematically in the following way:

$$7\times\left(+\frac{1}{3}+\frac{1}{4}+\frac{1}{5}+\frac{1}{6}+\frac{1}{7}\right) = 7\times\frac{153}{140} \doteqdot 7\times 1.09 = 7.63$$

[note: 7.63 is a number between 7 and 8. Cf. "seven" // "eight"]

37 For this literary technique in the literatures of the ancient Near East, see U. Cassuto, *From Adam to Noah* (Jerusalem, 1944, 1961), pp. 89 ff. [on Gen. 1 & 2]; K. A. Kitchen, *Ancient Orient and Old Testament* (Chicago, 1966), p. 117 [on Karnak Poetical Stela & Gebel Barkal Stela]; I. M. Kikawada, *Iraq* 45 (1983), pp. 43–45 [on Atra-Ḫasīs Epic.].

38 Fensham also notes the similar structure. According to him, "lines 10–25 form a unity. It is initiated by the description of Keret's impoverishment and from line 22 this same subject is again taken up. We have here a poem with an introduction in general terms of Keret's impoverishment and also a conclusion with a similar statement. The particulars of the calamities which caused this impoverishment are enumerated in the body of the poem. We may call it an inclusive poem, a neat piece of poetic imagery." (*JNSL* 1, pp. 21–22).

39 According to the present writer's analysis, KTU 1.17 / UT 2 Aqht I:1–5 is a ⟨general outline⟩ while I:5 ff. is a ⟨detailed description⟩. Note that the two-line parallelisms,

(1. 2–3) *uzr.ilm.yḷḥm.*
[uzr.yšqy.]bn.qdš

and

(1. 3–5) *yd /[ṣth.yᶜl.]wyškb.*
yd /[mizrth.]pyln

in the ⟨general outline⟩ are "expanded" in the ⟨detailed description⟩:

(1. 6–8, 9–11, 11–13) *uzr.ilm.dnil.*
uzr.ilm.ylḥm.
uzr.yšqy.bn.qdš

and

(1. 13–15) *yd.ṣth /[dn]il.*
yd.ṣth.yᶜl.wyškb.
[yd.]mizrth.pyln.

The ⟨general outline⟩ mentions briefly the destruction of the "royal house" (*bt mlk*) which had "seven" // "eight" sons. The destruction of the royal house means to the king Keret that his offspring (*ḥtk*) is ruined and his dynasty finished. Then, the ⟨detailed description⟩ of this motif follows. As a preliminary step, his legitimate wife (*aṯt.ṣdqh // mtrḫt.yšrh*) who gave birth to "seven" // "eight" sons "departed" (*tbʿt*):[40] i.e. loss of wife or *widowhood.* Then the real trouble comes – the death of the "total" number of his sons, which is more crucial than the loss of the king's wife or even the death of the king himself.[41] This state of *childlessness* is expressed emphatically in ll. 24–25 as the complete destruction of his entire "heir" (*yrṯ*).

Now, it should be noted that these two stages of loss, i.e. loss of wife (*widowhood*) and loss of children (*childlessness*), are not mentioned here accidentally. It was presumably the work of the god of Death in the Ugaritic society that brought about the destruction of the "royal house", even though no mention is made of the god Mot in this section of the Epic. The twofold function of the god of Death is symbolically represented by the two staffs, or weapons, which the god Mt-w-Šr holds in his hands,[42] the staff of widowhood (*ulmn*) and the staff of childlessness (*ṯkl*), in the ritual portion of the text KTU 1.23/UT 52, which is concerned with the fertility (i.e. life) of the land and society of Ugarit. The complete destruction of this god of Death was the prerequisite for the birth of the fertility gods, *ilm nʿmm*, which is described in the mythological portion of the text. Thus, the complete destruction of the deity who is in charge of the loss of wife and children brought about the "gain" of "two" wives and "seven" sons in KTU 1.23/UT 52.[43]

In the light of the above analysis, KTU 1.14:I / UT Krt: 10–11 is probably better to be grouped with the ⟨general outline⟩, ll. 1–11, rather than taking lines 10–25 as an "inclusive poem" as Fensham does (see note 38 above).

40 Whether this means the death of Keret's initial wife or her temporal departure does not matter for the present discussion on the state of widowhood. Cf. Gordon, *PLMU*, p. 35.

41 Note that the "total" death of Keret's sons is climactically described by the use of numeral *mšbʿt* as well as the particle *hn* "lo!" right before the expression, "by the sword" (*bšlḥ*), which signifies the death by the hand of enemy – the most tragic death as illustrated by David's word in II Sam. 24:14. [See also Rummel, *RSP* 3, p. 304 & no. 12] Emphasis on the present line might also be expressed by the existence of a "monocolon" here.

42 D. T. Tsumura, "A Ugaritic God, *MT-W-ŠR*, and his Two Weapons (UT 52:8–11)," *UF* 6 (1974), pp. 407–413; Cyrus H. Gordon, "Two Aramaic Incantations," in Gary A. Tuttle (ed.), *Biblical and Near Eastern Studies: Essays in Honor of W. S. LaSor* (Grand Rapids, 1978), pp. 234–237. See N. Wyatt's response to the present writer's identification of *Mt-w-Šr* with the god of death ["The Identity of *Mt w Šr*," *UF* 9 (1977), pp. 379–381], though I am not convinced by his explanataion.

43 See Tsumura, *The Ugaritic Drama*, pp. 222–227.

Whatever the relationship between KTU 1.23/UT 52 and the Keret Epic may be,[44] the problem of the "loss" and "gain" of children seems to be more crucial than the "loss" and "gain" of wife. The latter might be only a preliminary stage which, in the case of Keret Epic, leads to the state of childlessness and hence the destruction of the royal dynasty. As a human experience, the loss of children in widowhood seems to be the most disasterous one as illustrated in the other royal "epics" such as the Book of Ruth in the Old Testament and others.[45] For this reason I would rather find in the initial section of the Keret Epic the motif of "childlessness" as the results of widowhood and the subsequent loss of children. Hence, the position [A], i.e.

Keret has no heir because of the death of all his children after his legitimate wife "departed",

seems once more to be the better supported.

44 According to C. M. Foley's recent study, *The Gracious Gods and the Royal Ideology of Ugarit* (McMaster Univ., 1980), the Sitz im Leben of KTU 1.23 / UT 52 is "a royal liturgy designed to ensure the well-being of royal figures." Cf. *Newsletter for Ugaritic Studies* 23 (Dec., 1980), p. 5.

45 See also Isaiah 47:8–9, Hos 9:12, Jer 15:7–8, 18:21 etc.

Z. Weisman (University of Haifa, Israel)

THE PROPHETIC PATTERN OF ANOINTING KINGS IN ANCIENT ISRAEL*

We encounter the prophet as King-maker in the stories of the anointing of Saul and David to Kingship. Both stories follow the same pattern: a) A divine instruction to the prophet precedes the anointing (1 Sam 9,15–16; 16,1 ff.). b) The anointing is performed by a prophet (ibid. 10,1; 16,13), by pouring oil on the head of the designate king. c) It comes as a surprise to the designate (ibid. 9,21 b; 16,11). d) It is carried out at an occasional place where the designate happens to be, and not necessarily in a sanctuary. e) It involves privacy (1 Sam 9,26–27), or at least secrecy (1 Sam 16,2 ff.). f) It is followed by the sudden appearance of the Spirit of God upon the anointed (ibid. 10,6,10; 16,13). There are, of course, literary differences between the two stories concerning the way that these elements were applied, but basically they present the same ritual pattern and same concept as far as the divine choice of the king is concerned. In both, the anointing signifies their nomination and designation to become kings over God's people as distinct from the historical accounts of their public installation by the people themselves. (See 1 Sam 11, 15 LXX on Saul; 2 Sam 2,4.7; 5,3.17, cf. 1 Chr 11,3; 14,8 on David).

The main elements of this pattern can be discerned in the anointing of Jehu (2 Kgs 9). The act of his anointing to kingship is performed by one of 'the sons of the prophets' who was sent by Elisha to fulfill a previous divine instruction to Elijah (1 Kgs, 19,16). The anointing is performed in the same way, by pouring oil on the head of the designate-king. It comes as a surprise to the nominee. It is conducted in a very discreet manner. The anointing is accompanied by the proclamation of a divine commission which binds Jehu's nomination by the Lord to become "king over israel" with a specific mission to which he is summoned. However, unlike the anointings of Saul and David, there is no clear-cut differentiation in the anointing of Jehu between his divine designation and his public installation. Nor is there any indication that the Spirit of God appeared upon him following his anointing, as in the prophetic anointings of Saul and David.

* This paper is based on my study on "the Anointing as a Motif in the Making of the Charismatic King", that was published in *Biblica* 57 (1976). The revised paper concentrates on the Prophetic Pattern of Anointing kings in Ancient Israel. This pattern is investigated from the typological and ideological points of view as reflected from inner-biblical evidence.

Considering this pattern as a whole and the specific role which the prophet plays in it, it seems possible to assume that we are dealing here with a "prophetic" pattern of the anointing of kings. The fact that the verb "anoint" is used also in the nomination of Prophets, as is the case in the divine instruction to Elijah to anoint Elisha as his successor (1 Kgs 19,16); or the massage of the later Isaiah, (Isa. 61,1): "The Spirit of the lord God is upon me, because the Lord has anointed me", could only confirm this conclusion.[1]

Parallel to, or even in contradistinction with these prophetic-stories of the anointing of kings, we encounter also historical accounts. In these historical accounts, including those of the anointing of Saul and David, which have already been mentioned, the phrase 'anoint king over' ... denotes the people's installation of the king. This meaning seems to be implied in the reminiscence about the anointing of Abshalom (2 Sam 19,10). In the anointing of Jehoahaz, where this phrase is followed by "made him king" (2 Kgs 23,30), this refers clearly to a public rite of his installation. Details concerning this public rite appear in the account of the enthronement of Solomon (1 Kgs, 32–39) and Joash (2 Kgs 13, cf. 2 Chr 23) both from the House of David[2]. It is clear from these accounts that the anointing formed an essential rite in the public ceremony of their enthronement. Leaving out some minor divergences between the two we may outline major elements of that ceremony: a) It was a public ceremony. b) It was performed in a sacred place. (The anointing of Joash took place in the Temple of Jerusalem). c) The king was anointed by the priest (Joash by the high priest). The reference to 'Nathan the prophet' in the anointing of Solomon (1 Kgs 1,) in addition to Zadok the priest, who is the only one mentioned as the anointer in v. 39, is considered by many critics as an interpolation.[3] d) This was followed by the blowing of trumpets and the acclamation of the king by his attendants. e) In the story of Joash his coronation is explicitly mentioned (2 Kgs 11).

This pattern differs in structure and in function from the "prophetic" one. It is a public ceremony of inauguration and coronation conducted by the high officials of the people on their behalf, which entrusts the king with the legal authority, *de jure* and *de facto*, to reign over them. I dare not suggest, that the two different patterns represent two entirely opposite systems concerning the kingship in

1 The employment of the verb משח in the reference to prophets is considered by some scholars to be merely metaphorical! See: H. Weinel *ZAW* 18 (1898) p. 56; C. R. North *ZAW* 50 (1932), p. 13; E. Kutsch, *Salbung als Rechtsakt* (BZAW 87) 1963 p. 62 n. 235; G. Fohrer *AThANT* 31, 1957 p. 38f.

2 The Talmud differentiates between 'transitory reign' מלכות עוברת and 'everlasting reign' מלכות קיימת, which is referred to the House of David. According to the Talmud (Yer. Shekalim 49.3, Horayoth 47.3) only the first king has to be anointed, but not his son, unless there is a dispute about the successor.

3 See Weinel, *ibid* p. 24; J. Gray *1&2 Kings*, 1964, p. 90.

ancient Israel; but no doubt they represent two different aspects and outlooks. The first is concerned mainly with the teleological aspect of kingship, the king as the one who was chosen by God to function as his agent and who was summoned to fulfil a definite historical mission. This is evident in the anointings of Saul and Jehu, and it can also be assumed from the divine promise to David that by his hand God will save Israel from the hands of the Philistines, which is related to his anointing by the elders of Israel (2Sam 3,18 cf. 5,2–3). The second is mainly concerned with the legal aspect of kingship; the king *vis-a-vis* the people, his citizens.

The contradistinction between the two raises the question whether, or not, they both originated from one and the same "primary" pattern, and if originally they were interrelated to one another?

In fact, as far as cross-cultural examination goes one may find evidence for the use of anointing in the installation of kings in various historical records, some of which are older than the biblical sources; but none of these bears direct evidence of the implication of the anointing as a prophetic rite in the designation of kings. It seems, therefore, reasonable to assume that the rite of anointing in the "prophetic" pattern was transferred from some other context.

This in itself, suggests that we should look for parallels in which the anointing is employed as a rite of designation. And, indeed, there are records in which this function is evident. I refer particularly to the letter of Pharaoh Amen-ḥotep the third to the king of Arzawa (1411–1357 B.C.).[4] In his letter Pharaoh informs the king of Arzawa about a messenger who is sent by him to see his daughter, whom Pharaoh intends to make his wife, and to pour oil on her head. From the typological point of view there is a striking parallel, both in function and formula, between this communication and the divine instruction to the prophet to anoint David (1Sam 16,1) and Jehu (2Kgs 9,1.5.6). In both the messenger is sent by his Lord on a special mission to see the designate, to the place where the designate happens to be, and to pour oil on his head in order to sanctify him for his nomination.

The fact that the marriage-custom in the ancient Near East consisted of two stages, the first of which was the "betrothal",[5] might cast some light on the "Sitz im Leben" of the anointing as an act of designation. The "betrothal" was only the first act in this process, and had no binding force unless the marriage was completed by other acts. I venture to suggest that basically a similar concept underlines the relationship between the double "anointing" of Saul and David, and to a certain extent that of Jehu. According to this concept the position of the

4 EA 31. 11–14, J. A. Knudtzon, *Die El-Amarna Tafeln*, 1915 p. 271.

5 The "Inchoate marriage"; See G. R. Driver & J. C. Miles, *The Babylonian Laws* I (1952) p. 322ff.

anointed king had binding force only after he had been anointed in a public ceremony. In the meantime – between his secret nomination and his actual inauguration – he has to demonstrate his personal qualifications by undergoing a period of initiation and trial. This assumption may well suit the reasoning which Samuel adopted in his confrontation with Saul, in which the latter's divine nomination was withdrawn and he was rejected from being King over Israel. The excuse given is that Saul failed to fulfil one of the tasks to which he was commissioned in his nomination by the Lord (cf. 1Sam 13,13–14 with 10,8).

This typological affinity in itself does not necessarily give historical evidence for the anointing of Israelite kings by prophets prior to their installation; nevertheless, the possibility remains that in principle there could have been two different rites of anointing of kings, which in certain historical circumstances were performed successively: the first to nominate him, the second to install him publicly in his office.

It is beyond dispute among OT scholars that the second had taken place in the Israelite monarchy, although there is no decisive evidence that all the Israelite kings were actually anointed, or had to be anointed. There is no certainty, however, about the authenticity of the first. Moreover, being legendary most scholars tend to regard it as a "Theologumenon" which was projected from the public ceremony back to the "prophetic" one. It is not our purpose to argue about the historicity of the first (in the way which it is conveyed in the legends). However, the differences between the two patterns, both in structure and in function, make it almost impossible to regard the first as a later projection of the second. Apart from the anointing itself which was performed in different forms, in different places, and by different agents, there is not much in common between the two.

As far as ideology goes the "prophetic" pattern represents the idea of the "charismatic king" who is chosen, by God, as occasion required, to function as His commissioner in the political arena. This is underlined by the sudden appearance of the Spirit of Yahweh upon the anointed which follows this rite. The immediate cause of the manifestation of the king's extraordinary qualities was conceived to be not the magical rite of anointing, but the appearance of the "Spirit of Yahweh" upon him. This is clearly the case in the narratives of Saul, when he first emerges to save the people of Jabesh-gilead from the hands of the Ammonites (1Sam 11,6ff.).

In this respect there is no conceptual difference between the divine nomination of the saviour-king and the divine nomination of the saviour-judge (Jgs 6,11ff.; 13,2ff.). Both types are considered charismatic in biblical historiography. Moreover, even the stylistic formulation of the imparting of the "Spirit of God" upon them coincides. The only difference between the two divine nominations is in the implyment of a ritual or symbolic act which precedes the manifestation of the spirit upon the designate. In the "call" pattern of the saviour-judges we encounter the communication by the Theophanic Angel (such as in the stories of Gideon and Samson), whereas in the "call" pattern of the saviour-king we encounter the anointing by the "Man of God".[6] And, indeed, all the prophets who were involved in the anointing of the "charismatic" kings were also designated as "Man of God": Samuel – 1 Sam 9,7 ff.; Elija – 1 Kgs 17,18; 2 Kgs 1,9 ff.; Elisha – 2 Kgs 4,7 ff.; 5,8.; 6,6 ff.; 7,2 ff.; 13,19.

This brings us to the last phase of our investigation, namely the affinity between the anointing and the imparting of the spirit upon the anointed. The question whether this connection is original, can hardly be answered definitely; as there is abundant anthropological data in which similar phenomenological affinities are overt, yet, cannot be historically substantiated.

Most of the examples, in the anthropological data related to the connection between the anointing and the "mana" can hardly correspond to the prophetic pattern, either because of the public aspect of this rite which does not single out the individual, or because they lack the element of the divine nomination. However, one may similarly detect an affinity between the "anointing" and the "possession" by the spirit in some shamanistic rituals. It is worthwhile to quote here from Williams and Colvert's account of the Fijians who consult the oracle:[7] "... Sometimes there is placed before the priest a dish of scented oil, with which he anoints himself ... the priest becomes absorbed in thought ... in a few minutes he trembles ... these increase to violent muscular action ... In some instances this is accompanied with murmurs and sobs ... the priest is now possessed by god, and all his words and actions [are] considered as no longer his own, but those of the deity who has entered into him" ...

Obviously one can recall some similarities to this account in the story of Saul (1 Sam 10,9 ff.; cf. 19,23–24); however, the functional as well as the conceptual differences between the two cannot be denied. The anointing of Saul by Samuel represents a prophetic, symbolic act rather than a magical one, which is self-performed. It is concerned with his divine nomination rather than with the faculty of consulting the deities. The bestowal of the Spirit of Yahweh upon him symbolizes the transcendental effect upon the "possessed" rather than the animistic.

Whether or not one may assume that in the "prophetic" pattern an archaic survival of a magical rite has been incorporated, there can be no doubt that it has undergone radical modifications as a result of the new religious and culture context in which it was incorporated. The transformation of the magical rite of

6 Z. Weisman, *The Charismatic Personality in the OT* (unpublished diss. 1972).
7 T. W. Williams and J. Calvert, *Fiji and the Fijians* I (1858) p. 224 f.

anointing to a prophetic symbolic act and its attachment to the "call" pattern signifies the Israelite prophetic ideology. This ideology reflects the ambivalent attitude of the prophets towards the kingship in Israel. On the one hand, there is the fear that the Israelite kingship will be like that of other nations, and that by their demand to establish a kingship the Israelites reject the Lord "from being king over them" (1 Sam 8,5 ff.). On the other hand, there is the necessity to comply with the people's will to replace the rule of the judges (ibid. 8,1 ff.) by an efficient national rule (ibid. 8,20). These conflicting tendencies were reconciled in this prophetic pattern of the anointing of kings. The imparting of the 'Spirit of Yahweh' upon the king depicted his charisma as the people's saviour, who delivers the people from the hand of their enemies, similar to that of the Judge-Saviour. The symbolic rite of anointing by the prophet depicted the king's institutional authority. This authority is reflected in the words of Samuel to Saul: "Though you are little in your own eyes, are you not the head of the tribes of Israel? The Lord anointed you king over Israel" (1 Sam 15,17).

The reconcilation between the two conflicting tendencies towards the monarchy in Israel, may explain the employment of the prophetic anointing in the nomination of the first king in Israel. After the establishment of the monarchy in Israel we find the prophet as king-maker and anointer only in the nomination of kings in the Northern Kingdom. There is no indication, however, to the prophet's role as king-maker in the Davidic Kingdom in Judah. Moreover, in the two cases mentioned before, where kings from the House of David were anointed (Solomon and Joash) the anointing was performed by the priest, in a public ceremony of their inauguration.

Whether or not a distinction between two opposing monarchial systems could be made, one charismatic which prevailed in the Northern Kingdom, and the other hereditary-dynastic which prevailed in Judah, as was suggested by Alt[8], should be left to further investigations.

8 A. Alt, "Das Königtum in dem Reiche Israel und Juda" *VT 1* (1951) pp. 2–22.

YUTAKA IKEDA (Ibaraki Christian College)

HITTITES AND ARAMAEANS IN THE LAND OF BIT-ADINI

After the fall of the Hittite Empire, about 1200 B.C., the Aramaeans arose from the Syrian desert and played a dominant role in the history of Syria for several generations.[1] Still, the descendants of the Hittites, or as they are generally called, the Neo-Hittites, did survive the turmoil of the last stages of the Late Bronze Age of the Near East and indeed succeeded in establishing their own states in parts of northern Syria. Even the Assyrians and other people of Mesopotamia continued to call northern Syria the "land of Hatti" and its residents "Hittites".[2]

Not surprisingly, northern Syria became a place of cultural and political confrontation as well as a place of co-existence for the surviving Indo-European Hittites and the rising West-Semitic Aramaeans. One of the prominent examples of this historical phenomenon is the case of Bit-Adini, the state on the Euphrates which Shalmaneser III describes as having done "bold and violent deeds against the kings my fathers". Indeed Bit-Adini was the great enemy of Shalmaneser III until it was finally destroyed by him and subsequently rebuilt as the most important province of the Assyrian Empire at the gate of the west (in 855 B.C.).[3]

The Aramaean character of Bit-Adini seems to be indicated by the form of the name, which contains DUMU/Bit,[4] and also by the form of the personal name of

1 See A. Malamat, "The Aramaeans," in D. J. Wiseman (ed.), *Peoples of Old Testament Times*, London 1973 (= *POTT*), pp. 134ff.; H. Tadmor, "The Decline of Empires in Western Asia ca. 1200 B.C.E," in F. M. Cross (ed.), *Symposia Cellebrating the Seventy-fifth Anniversary of the Founding of the American Schools of Oriental Research (1900–1975)*, Cambridge MA 1979, pp. 1ff.

2 See J. D. Hawkins, "Assyrians and Hittites," *Iraq* 36 (1974), 68; idem, *RLA* IV (1972), 152 s.v. Hatti, and the same author's latest studies concerning the general history of the Neo-Hittite states in Syria and Anatolia (*The Cambridge Ancient History* [= *CAH*] III/1 Cambridge 1982, Chapter 9).

3 E. Michel, "Die Assur-Texte Salmanassars III. (858–824)," *WO* 2 (1954–59), 414f.; D. D. Luckenbill, *Ancient Records of Assyria and Babylonia*, New York 1968 (reprint) [= *ARAB*] I, § 608. The same expression can also be found in the recently found Kenk Gorge inscription of Shalmaneser III (O. A. Taşyürek, "A Rock Relief of Shalmaneser III of the Euphrates," *Iraq* 41 (1979), 48f.).

4 The component suggests the tribal structure of the state, at least in its early stages of development. Cf. J. A. Brinkman, *A Political History of Post-Kassite Babylonia 1158–722 B.C.*, Rome 1968, [= *PHPKB*] pp. 255, 264, 266; T. Ishida, *The Royal Dynasties in Ancient Israel*, Berlin–New York 1977, pp. 102f.

the last king of Bit-Adini, Ahuni (i.e. "our brother"). However, the Hieroglyphic Luwian Inscriptions on the reliefs from Tell Ahmar (i.e. the ancient Til-Barsip, or the last royal stronghold of Ahuni,[5] circa 900 B.C.) on the east bank of the Euphrates undeniably prove the existence of Hittite dynasts in Til-Barsip before Ahuni's reign.[6] This suggests that Bit-Adini was not exclusively Aramaean in nature.

Most recently, new editions of the Hieroglyphic Luwian inscriptions on the more important of the two stelae from Tell Ahmar (Tell Ahmar 1) and those on the stele Aleppo 2 have been published by J. D. Hawkins.[7] Thanks to these editions based upon collated texts we can now describe with much greater accuracy the rule of those Hittite dynasts of Til-Barsip. It is the purpose of this paper to reconsider the political climate of the land of Bit-Adini and its Hittite-Aramaean interconnections in the tenth and first half of the ninth century B.C.

The name Bit-Adini is first attested in the inscriptions of Adad-nerari II (911–891 B.C.). On the occasion of the king's military campaign against the land of Hanigalbat in 899 B.C., a shipment of female apes was sent to him as a tribute from the land Bit-Adini (KUR DUMU *A-di-ni*).[8] It is not certain exactly when the Aramaean state Bit-Adini was established.[9] A suggestion has been made relating the establishment of Bit-Adini with the conquest of the Assyrian colonies Pitru and Mutkinu by a king of the land of Aram during the reign of Ashur-rabi II (ca. 1013–933 B.C.) as recounted in the Kurkh Monolith of Shalmaneser III.[10]

5 For the different titles given for Til-Barsip in the inscriptions of Shalmaneser III, see Y. Ikeda, "Royal Cities and Fortified Cities," *Iraq* 41 (1979), 77–79.

6 For the iconographical investigation of the Tell Ahmar reliefs and their possible date, see D. Ussishkin, "Was Bit-Adini a Neo-Hittite or Aramaen State?," *Orientalia* 40 (1971), 433; J. D. Hawkins, 'The "Autobiography of Ariyahinas's Son": An Edition of the Hieroglyphic Luwian Stelae Tell Ahamar 1 and Aleppo 2,' *AnSt* 30 (1980), 155f. W. Orthmann, *Untersuchungen zur spätethitischen Kunst*, Bonn 1971 [= *USHK*], pp. 46–48, 184; H. Genge, *Nordsyrisch-sudanatolische Reliefs* I–II, København 1979 [= *NSR*], pp. 53–55, 94.

7 *AnSt* 30, 139ff.

8 A. K. Grayson, *Assyrian Royal Inscriptions*, Wiesbaden 1976 [= *ARI* 2], § 426. Such tribute was not as strange as it may sound, even though apes are not native to northern Syria. No doubt the rulers of Bit-Adini purchased them from Egypt. Collections of rare and strange animals were not unusual among the rulers of the Ancient Near East, especially in the period of 12th–9th centuries B.C. For a more detailed discussion of this matter, see Y. Ikeda, "Solomon's Trade in Horses and Chariots in Its International Setting," in T. Ishida (ed.). *Studies in the Period of David and Solomon and Other Essays*, Tokyo 1982, [= *EPDS*] pp. 218ff.

9 For the development of this problem see the classical discussion by B. Landberger, *Sam'al* I, Ankara 1948, pp. 35f.

10 *ARAB* I § 603. See J.-R. Kupper, *Les nomades en Mesopotamie au temps des rois de Mari*, Paris 1957, p. 122; Ussishkin *Orientalia* 40, 432, 437.

It should be noted, however, that though the Kurkh Monolith repeatedly refers to Bit-Adini and its cities, the conquest of Pitru and Mutkinu is described merely as having been accomplished by a king of the land of Aram (*šar* KUR *A-ru-mu*) and not by the ruler of Bit-Adini *per se*.

In the Old Testament the term "Aram" is employed in general reference to the Aramaeans in Syria, but it is also used more precisely as the appellative for the Aramaean state in the south which had Damascus as its centre. The ruler of Aram-Damascus is always called there the "king of Aram" and is referred to as such in the Aramaic inscriptions of Bar-Hadad and of Zakur (*mlk 'rm*).[11] The Assyrian equivalent for the Old Testament "Damascus" (Biblical Hebrew *dammeśeq*) is *Dimašqu* (URU *Dimašqa/i/u*), but the state Aram-Damascus is always given the name *Ša-imēri-šú* lit. "the city of his ass" (KUR *Ša* ANŠE-*šú*, *Ša* KUR ANŠE-*šú*, KUR *I-me-ri*, KUR ANŠE-*šú*), not Aram.[12]

The plural form KUR *A-ri/a-mi/e* (MEŠ) in the Assyrian inscriptions implies the Aramaean tribes in general; indeed, the Assyrians used the geographical name KUR *Arumu* in this same general sense to indicate the broad extent of land on "this side of the Euphrates," as the east bank of the river is often called, which was predominantly settled by the Aramaeans.

The usage of the term KUR *Arumu* should be contrasted to the usage of KUR *Ḫatti* (the land of Hatti) for northern Syria on "the other side of the Euphrates," (i.e. the west bank of the river) which refers, primarily, to the land of Carchemish, but also to other states.[13] Tiglath-pileser I (1116–1076 B.C.) claims that he pursued after the *aḫlamē*-Aramaeans along the Euphrates and plundered "from the edge of the land Suhu to the city Carchemish of the land Hatti,"[14] a definition of the land densely populated by the Aramaeans – the "land of Aram" (or "Aram-Naharaim," to use the biblical equivalent for the great Bend of the Euphrates).[15] The land of Aram (KUR *A-ru-mu*) is referred to in the inscriptions of Ashur-dan II (934–912 B.C.) in connection with the Aramaean conquest of the Assyrian territories which occured during his lifetime.[16]

11 For the proposal to identify *šar* KUR *Arumu* of Kurkh Monolith with Hadadezer, king of Aram-zobah, the contemporary of David of Israel, see Malamat, *POTT*, p. 142; idem, „Das davidische und salomonische Königreich und seine Beziehungen zu Ägypt und Syrien. Zur Entstehung eines Großreichs", *Österreichische Akademie der Wissenschaften Philosophisch-historische Klasse. Sitzungsberichte* 407 (1983), 37–39, and see most recently Hawkins, *CAH* III/1, pp. 381f. For the reading Zakur in place of the former Zakir, see J. D. Hawkins, *RLA* V 239 s. v. Jaḫan; A. R. Millard, "Epigraphic Notes, Aramaic and Hebrew," *PEQ* 110 (1978), 23.

12 Ikeda, *Iraq* 41, 81.

13 For this matter see Hawkins, *RLA* IV, 153f.

14 *ARI* 2 §§ 34, 70, 143.

15 Concerning this geographical concept see J. J. Finkelstein, "Mesopotamia", *JNES* 26 (1962), 73ff.

16 *ARI* 2 §§ 363, 388 and n. 321. Cf. Hawkins, *RLA* V 238f.

In the course of time a number of the roving Aramaean tribes consolidated their rule around fortified cities in order to be more "state-like". About this same time the Assyrians began to designate the regions inhabited by the Aramaeans by their local geographical or tribal names in place of the more general KUR *Arumu*. Still, these Aramaean "states" were only loosely organized,[17] and thus Adad-nerari II recounts receiving tribute from the land Suhu and from the land Bit-Adini without mentioning any specific name of their rulers.[18] It is therefore possible that the term "land of Bit-Adini" (KUR DUMU *Adini*) here is used generally in a geographical, not political, sense, to indicate the northern part of the land of Aram as opposed to lands such as Laqu and Suhu in the south.[19]

In the time of Ashur-naṣir-apli II (883–859 B.C.) the residents of the city Suru in the land of Laqu on the Habur murdered Hamataya ("the Hamathite"), the governor of the city, in rebellion against Assyria (883 B.C.), and a man called Ahi-yababa became their king. Ashur-naṣir-apli's reaction was swift and decisive. Ahi-yababa was captured and all the guilty citizens were severely punished.[20]

Ahi-yababa is described as a "son of nobody (the Assyrian terminology means 'usurper'), whom they brought from Bit-Adini." Yet, it is not clear that Ahi-yababa himself was a man of Bit-Adini. Neither is it certain that the Assyrians assumed that Bit-Adini was directly responsible for the revolt of the inhabitants of Suru who supported Ahi-yababa, for no name of the ruler of Bit-Adini, who might otherwise have been blamed for the anti-Assyrian move, is given.[21]

Ashur-naṣir-apli II appointed Azi-ili, the Laqean, as the new governor of Suru. But Azi-ili, being ambitious himself, dared, after five years, to break his oath of allegiance to the overlord of Assyria. Trusting in "his own might," and allied with other Laqean leaders (like Hemti-ili and Ila), Azi-ili engaged a fierce battle with the Assyrian troops at the crossing of the Euphrates near the city Kipinu. Azi-ili, recognizing the failure of the revolt, fled along the Euphrates to Mount Bisuru (mod. Jebel Bishri) and then as far as the cities Dummetu and Azumu, "cities of Bit-Adini." Ashur-naṣir-apli II was greatly chagrined in having to admit that Azi-ili had "vanished" safely from the mass of the Assyrian army pursuing after him.[22] The land of Bit-Adini again had become a haven for the anti-Assyrian elements on the Habur.

17 On this issue see Ikeda, *Iraq* 41, 76 and footnote 9.

18 *ARI* 2, §§ 421, 426. See also Ikeda, *Iraq* 41, 76 and n. 9; A. R. Millard and P. Bordreuil, "A statue from Syria with Assyrian and Aramaic Inscription," *BA* Summer 1982, 138f.

19 For the description of these lands see *ARI* 2 §§ 471–473, 579.

20 *ARI* 2 § 547. On Hamataya ("Hamathite") see also below footnote 32.

21 For arguments in support of Bit-Adini's having made direct interference in the rebellion of Suru, see A. K. Grayson, "Studies in Neo-Assyrian History. The Ninth Century B.C.", *BiOr* 33 (1976), 136; Hawkins, *AnSt* 30, 148.

22 *ARI* 2, §§ 579–580; Grayson, *BiOr* 33, 139.

Even if we assume that the Aramaeans of Bit-Adini had indeed already been active on the east bank of the Euphrates in the time of Ashur-rabi II, we may conclude from the detailed description above that by using the archaic geographical term "land of Aram," the scribe of the Kurkh Monolith clearly recognized the fact that the conqueror of Pitru and Mutkinu had not been a man of Bit-Adini.

However, just as the states in the land of Hatti were made up not only of Hittites but of non-Hittite inhabitants as well,[23] so the "land of Aram" was inhabited by non-Aramaean people along with the dominant Aramaeans. In the inscriptions of Ashur-naṣir-apli II, the ruler of Bit-Bahiani (with Guzana as its centre) is not called by his personal name but designated only as the "Hittite" (KUR *Ḫat-ta-a+a*),[24] an indication that he was not an Aramaean in origin. If W. F. Albright's suggestion concerning the title of Kapara is accepted,[25] then it is possible that Kapara, the king of Bit-Bahiani, called himself the "king of the land of Hatti (KUR *Hat-té-e*)." Even more important support for the concept of non-Aramaean inhabitants of the "land of Aram" may be seen in the knowledge we have of the Hittites of Til-Barsip.

It is in the inscriptions of Shalmaneser III (858–824 B.C.) that the name Til-Barsip is for the first time attested.[26] The name which was used by the Hittites of Til-Barsip to refer to their royal city or their state is not known, unfortunately, due to the corruption of the texts from Tell Ahmar. According to Tell Ahmar 1, Hapatila was the great-grandfather of Ariyahinas's son, author of the text. We are thus required to consider the dynastic line of the Hittites of Til-Barsip to have

23 For the states of mixed population such as Sam'al, Que and Hamath see B. Landsberger, *Sam'al*, pp. 12ff., 38ff.; J. D. Bing, *A History of Cilicia during the Assyrian Period*, (Ph. D. dissertation, Indiana University) Ann Arbor 1969, pp. 33ff.; Orthmann *USHK*, pp. 194ff., 199ff., 211ff.; Ussishkin, *Orientalia* 40, 437; Hawkins, *RLA* IV, 67–70 (s. v. Hamath) and idem, *CAH* III/1, 328ff.; Ikeda, *Iraq* 41, 79ff.

24 L. W. King, *Annals of the Kings of Assyria*, London 1902, 302:22; *ARI* 2, § 553.

25 W. F. Albright, "The Date of Kapara Period at Gozan (Tell Halaf)," *AnSt* 6 (1956), 82, whereas W. Röllig prefers to read KUR *Pa-le$_8$-e* (*RLA* V, 391 s. v. Kapara). The name Kapara can be related to the Hittite *Kapparaya* (E. Laroche, *Les noms de Hittites*, Paris 1966, no. 509); M. Liverani, "Antecendenti dell'onomastica aramaica antica," *RStOr* 37 (1962). 74; Genge, *NSR*, p. 127. Cf. the view labeling the name as Aramaic (Röllig, ibid.), and also Orthmann, *USHK*, 180 n. 24. For the recently published bilingual text of Adad-it'i, governor of Guzana, which is to be dated in the middle of the ninth century B.C., see A. Abou-Assaf, f. Bordreuil and A. Millard, *La statue de Tell Fekherye et son inscription bilingue assyro-arameenne*, Paris 1982; A. R. Millard, „Assyrians and Arameans," *Iraq* 45 (1983), 104f., and the article by Millard and Bordreuil referred to above in footnote 18. But it should also be noted that J. Naveh, based on Aramic paleography, proposes to push the date up to the 11th century B. C. ("The Date of the Inscription from Tell Fekherye," *Šnaton lamiqra' ulḥeqer hamizraḥ haqadum* V/VI 1983, 131–135 (Hebrew). Cf. also J. C. Greenfield and A. Shaffer, "Notes on the Akkadian-Aramaic Bilingual Statue from Tell Fekherye," *Iraq* 45 [1983], 109–116).

26 See *Iraq* 41, 78f., 87 Table II.

been in existence a century before Ariyahinas's son,[27] giving a possible dating for the reign of Hapatila around 1,000 B.C. If this was the case, Hapatila must have been the contemporary of Ashur-rabi II.

In fact, Hapatila exerted considerable power beyond the original borders of Til-Barsip as "he governed in the west and in the east" (Tell Ahmar 1:9).[28] Thus, for the local populace the Aramaeans were by no means the sole rulers of the east bank of the Euphrates. The Hittite rulers, too, were eager to expand their influence eastwards, never being content merely to watch idly as the Aramaeans increased their influence.

Hapatila is said to have died in the land of Anat (Tell Ahmar 1:10),[29] and it is most probable that the activities of the Hittites of Til-Barsip reached to Anat, midway down the Euphrates. Anat in the land Suhu had long been considered an important centre for international trade in the ancient Near East, and its seizure and control was crucial both for the Aramaeans and the Assyrians.[30]

The Tell Ahmar stele informs us of an additional political factor in the power struggle which took place in the reign of Hapatila: the Hittites on the Euphrates. It seems that the relations between the Hittites of Til-Barsip and the inhabitants of Anat somehow continued even after the reign of Hapatila, for Hamiyatas, son of Masuwarazas, the usurper of the Hapatila dynasty, says in his inscription: "During my (good) times I settled the Anatean . . ." (Tell Ahmar 2:6).[31] In this connection it should also be noted that the Hittite rulers of Hamath on the Orontes had a close relationship with the residents of the lands of Anat and Laqu during the second half of the 9th century B.C.[32]

27 Hawkins, *AnSt* 30, 155.

28 Ibid., 142.

29 Ibid.

30 Anat of the land of Suhu is repeatedly mentioned in the inscriptions of Tiglath-pileser I in connection with his pursuits after the Aramaeans (*ARI* 2, §§ 83, 97, 143) as well as in the text of Ashur-bel-kala (*ARI* 2, 261). In 885 B. C. Tukulti-Ninurta II received from Ilu-ibni, governor of the land of Suhu, a bountiful tribute made up of three talents of silver, 20 minas of gold, an ivory couch, three ivory chests, 18 tin bars, 40 furniture legs of *meskannu*-wood, a bed of *meskannu*-wood, six dishes of *meskannu*-wood, a bronze bathtub, linen garments, garments with multi-coloured trim, purple wool, oxen, sheep, bread and beer (*ARI* 2, § 471). Cf. J. A. Brinkman, *PHPKB* pp. 183ff.; N. B. Jankowska, "Some Problems of the Economy of the Assyrian Empire," in *Ancient Mesopotamia. Socio-Economic History*, Moscow 1969, p. 269.

31 Hawkins, *AnSt* 30, 147f.

32 H. Ingholt, *Rapport préliminaire sur sept campagnes de fouilles a Hama en Syrie (1932–38)*, København 1940, p. 115 n. 10; J. Laessøe *apud* E. Fugmann, *Hama. Fouilles et recherches de la fondation Carsberg 1932–1938*, København 1958, p. 190f. The land of Laqu is plausibly mentioned (*Laqawani*) in the Hieroglyphic Luwian inscription of Uratami, son of Urhilina, king of Hamath (Meriggi, *Manuale di eteo geroglifico* II/1 Rome 1967, no. 8). It is also possible that Hamath on the Orontes was related to "the Hamathite", a sheikh of Laqu in the inscription of

As recounted in the text of Ariyahinas's son, Hapatila governed not only an expanse of land on the east bank of the Euphrates, but also "in the west" – that is, in part of the land of Hatti on the west bank of the river. It is even tempting to assume that the "king of the land of Aram," conqueror of Pitru and Mutkinu, was none other than Hapatila of the Tell Ahmar stele.[33]

Til-Barsip is located only 20 km downstream from Carchemish (mod. Jerablus), the centre of the land of Hatti, and it is certain that culturally the two city-states Til-Barsip and Carchemish were very similar.[34] But it is not clear that there had always been close political ties between Til-Barsip and Carchemish, whose capitals stood on the opposite banks of the Euphrates and who were rivals for control of the important commercial routes between west and east. In the time of Hapatila, at least, the relation between the two Hittite states must have been far from amicable, partly because of the expansionism policy of the ruler of Til-Barsip in the land of Hatti.

It is possible that Tiglath-pileser I took Pitru (biblical Pethor), on the Sajur River, away from Carchemish to make it an Assyrian commercial and military strategic base on the west bank of the Euphrates.[35] But it may have been Hapatila of Til-Barsip – if the assumption that he was the contemporary of Ashur-rabi II is correct – who took it away from the Assyrians before the people of Carchemish

Tukulti-Ninurta II (W. Schramm, "Die Annalen des assyrischen Königs Tukulti-Ninurta II (890–884 v. Chr.)," *BiOr* 27 (1970), 152 Rs. 5 and "the Hamathite", the governor of Suru (above footnote 16). J. Lewy suggested that Zakur's attribute *'s ʿnh* should be interpreted as "man from Anat" ("Studies in the Historic Geography of the Ancient Near East," *Orientalia* 21, 1952, 415 n. 6, 418).

33 Cf. B. Landsberger once suggested that the conqueror of the cities Pitru and Mutkinu may not have been Aramaean (*Sam'al* I, p. 35, n. 74). For other views concerning the identification of the "king of the land of Aram", see above footnotes 8 and 9.

34 The strong resemblance between the reliefs of Tell Ahmar and those of Carchemish and their parallel stylistic development in the art of carving have been fully discussed (See above footnote 6). A few more points can be added: Not only that Kupapa, the goddess of Carchemish is found among the pantheon of Til-Barship (Tell Ahmar 1:2, Tell Ahmar 2:1, Aleppo 2:26. For the goddess Kubaba see recent study by J. D. Hawkins, "Kubaba at Karkamiš and Elsewhere", *AnSt* 31 (1981), 147ff.), but that the otherwise unattested ornamental title "country-king" (REGIO REX) of the dedicator of Tell Ahmar 1 corresponds to the title "country lord" (REGIO DOMINUS) common to the rulers of Carchemish (Hawkins, *AnSt* 30, 142). Furthermore, the title "judge" [("IUDEX") *tarwanis*] of Ariyahinas, father of the author of Tell Ahmar 1, is indeed another title common to the kings of Carchemish [Those are Suhis (ca. 960 B.C.), Katuwas (ca. 900 B.C.), Yariris (ca. 760 B.C.) and Kamanis (ca. 750 B.C.). E. Laroche, *Les hieroglyphes hittites* I, Paris 1960, 371. Hawkins, translating ("IUDEX") *tarwanis* as "ruler", assumes that the title was used by subordinate governor ("Some Historical Problems of the Hieroglyphic Luwian Inscriptions," *AnSt* 29, 1979, 157].

35 On the internal change of Carchemish toward the mid-10th century B.C. and its implication for the international trades of that era, see Y. Ikeda, *SPDS*, pp. 232f.

recovered it for themselves. It seems that after Hapatila, the power of the Hittite rulers became weaker until finally Til-Barsip itself fell to the Aramaean strong man Ahuni of Bit-Adini. Elsewhere we have argued that the Hittite Til-Barsip was an independent state and did not belong to the Aramaean state of Bit-Adini until its conquest by Ahuni.[36] This is in contrast to the view that the Hittite dynasty of Til-Barsip displaced, for nearly a century, the Aramaean dynasty of Bit-Adini.[37]

The name Ahuni is mentioned in the inscriptions of Ashur-naṣir-apli II[38] and it is possible that he reigned over the Aramaeans of Bit-Adini even during the time of Ashur-naṣir-apli's predecessor. Yet it was in the time of Shalmaneser III that Ahuni ceased to pay tribute and tax to the overlord of Assyria, breaking a custom which had been observed by the rulers of Bit-Adini before Ahuni and, for a while, by Ahuni himself (Kenk Gorge 8–9).[39] Moreover, we learn that Ahuni held not a few cities in the Hatti land, such as [ ]-ga, Tagi-[ ], Surunu, Paripa, Til-Bashre, Dabigu, and Nappigi.[40]

There is reason to assume that some parts of the region south of the Sajur River (e.g. Nappigi – mod. Membij) had been under the dominion of the Hittite rulers of Til-Barsip until they were "inherited" by Ahuni when he conquered the city state of Til-Barsip. Still, it was from the land of Carchemish that Ahuni took for himself the cities on the Queiq River such as Dabigu (mod. Dabiq).[41]

Ahuni and his contemporary Sangara king of Carchemish were allies in 858 B.C. when the mass of troops led by Shalmaneser III clashed with the forces of the anti-Assyrian coalition made up of the states of northern Syria.[42] This connection must have been, however, nothing but a temporary tie created out of urgency in the face of a common enemy of people who otherwise disputed over Ahuni's high handed policy to expand the territory of Bit-Adini in the land of Hatti. This enemy-colleague relationship is parallel to that between Ben-Hadad II (Adad-idri) of Damascus and Ahab of Israel who, in spite of unceasing rivaly and

36 *The Kingdom of Hamath and Its Relations with Aram and Israel* (Ph. D. Dissertation, The Hebrew University of Jerusalem 1977, in Hebrew), p. 95, and see now Hawkins, *AnSt* 30, 156.

37 Ussishkin, *Orientalia* 40, 437.

38 *ARI* 2 §§ 583–584.

39 Taşgürek, *Iraq* 41, 49.

40 *ARAB* I § 601. Cf. Ikeda, *Iraq* 41, 77f.

41 Hawkins, *PLA* IV, 154.

42 *ARAB* I § 599. For the coalition of the states of the northern Syria cf. E. G. H. Kraeling, *Aram and Israel*, New York 1918, pp. 68–71; W. W. Hallo, "From Qarqar to Carchemish: Assyria and Israel in the Light of New Discoveries," in D. N. Freedman and E. F. Campbell, Jr. (ed.), *The Biblical Archaeologist Reader*, 2 New York 1964 [= *BARd* 2], p. 159; J. D. Hawkins, *RLA* V 444 s. v. Karkamiš, and see also H. Tadmor, "Azriyau of Yaudi," *Scripta Hierosolymitana* VIII, 1961, 239ff.

repeated clashes of their troops, allied themselves at the head of the coalition of the states of southern Syria in the battle of Qarqar against Shalmaneser III in 853 B.C.[43]

In concluding: The latest editions of the Hieroglyphic inscriptions from Tell Ahmar and Aleppo shed new light on the relations of the Hittites of Til-Barsip with the people on both sides of the Euphrates; the new editions also better our understanding of the general political climate along the Euphrates of the tenth and first half of the ninth century B.C. A series of conflicts and confrontations between the Aramaeans and the Hittites, and amongst the Hittites themselves, and the Aram-Hittite alliance against the Assyrians best characterize this era.[44]

43 *ARAB* I § 601. For the battle of Qarqar see Malamat, *POTT*, PP. 143ff.; H. W. F. Saggs, "The Assyrians," in *POTT*, 159; Hallo, *BARd* 2, pp. 159–161; B. Mazar, "The Aramaean Empire and Its Relations with Israel," in *BARd* 2, pp. 137ff.; Ikeda, *Iraq* 41, 79ff.

44 I am grateful to Professor Hayim Tadmor for his helpful critical comments.

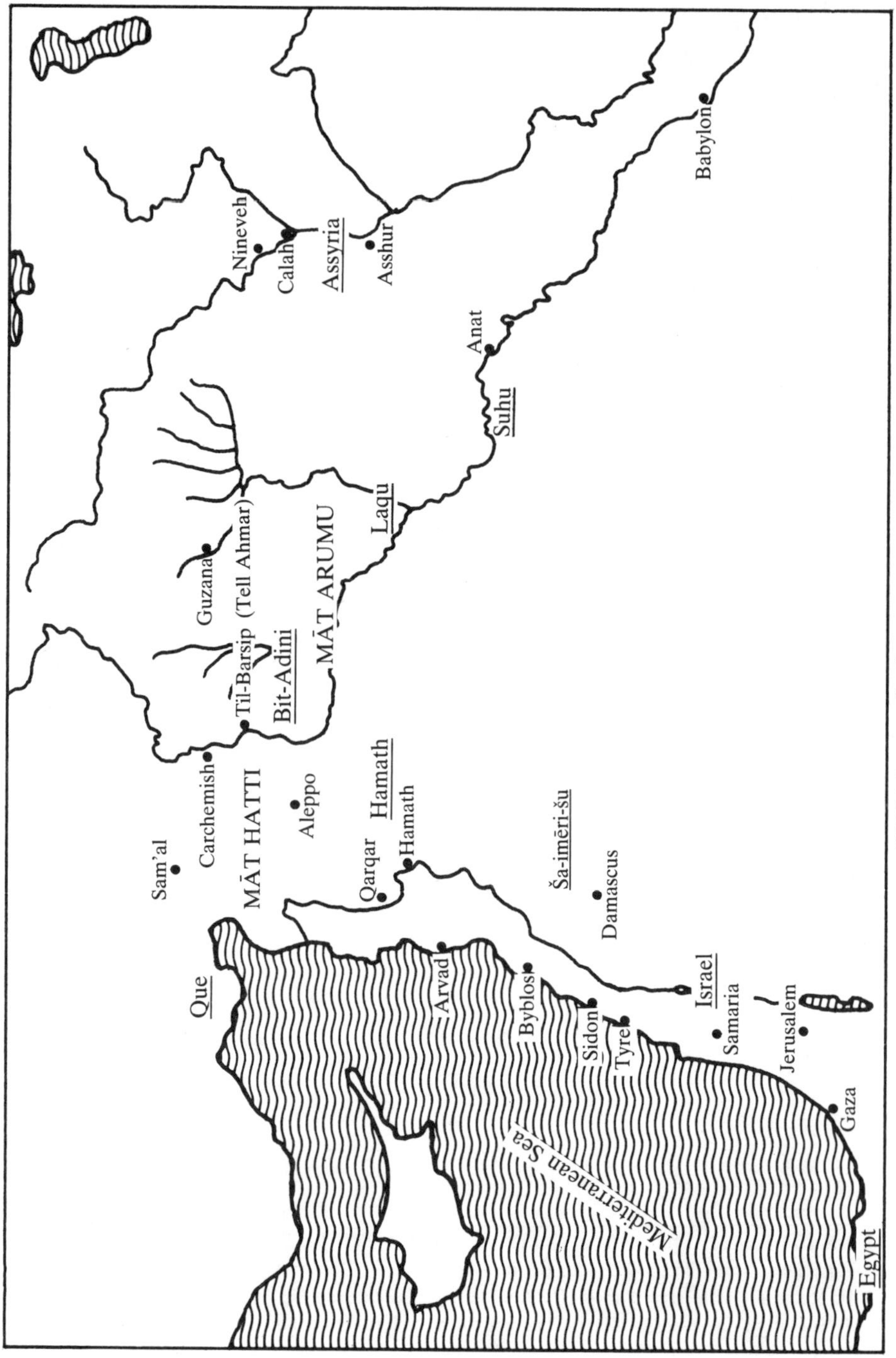

SYRIA in the 10th–9th centuries B. C.

Donald J. Wiseman (University of London)

PALACE AND TEMPLE GARDENS IN THE ANCIENT NEAR EAST

The abundant resources from Assyria and Babylonia have hitherto not been fully exploited for the information they yield on gardens. This is in part due to the difficulty of identifying technical terms for flora pending the updating of Campbell Thompson's *Dictionary of Assyrian Botany* (1948) by Franz Köcher's forthcoming study of plants listed in the lexical series.[1] Moreover, only a very few undisputed representations of gardens occur on the Assyrian sculptures[2], and these scarcely compare with the evidence of the Egyptian tomb paintings.[3]

At Nineveh Sennacherib laid out a 'large garden (*kirimāhu*) like Mt. Amānus beside his great palace'.[4] Since it was near a threshing floor it must have been raised high above the river which watered it. It lay close by the city walls and was reached by a special garden gate. Within it were planted all kinds of herbs (*riqqē*) and fruit-trees such as grow in mountain areas and Babylonia as well as rare plants.[5] These royal gardens were also said to contain trees, saplings and cuttings collected from diverse lands and mountain regions. Sennacherib's family connections meant that many of these plants came from the West, yet he claimed that they thrived larger and more fruitful than those grown in their natural habitat.[6] One area was allocated to wild-vines, exotic plants and aromatics and in another low-lying part, near a dam made to hold back the R. Khosr, swamp and aquatic plants were interspersed with pools and reeds to become the habitat of migrating birds, wild boars, fishes and aquatic animals. This appears to be part of a larger game-park (*ambassu*) used for hunting. The suggestion of Oppenheim that the palace garden was a mere small scale imitation of the extra-urban *ambassu* can be discounted in that the one is stated to be adjacent to the other.[7] In this Sennacherib c. 700 B.C. was following a long tradition for four hundred years before Tiglath-pileser I refers to his luxurious gardens and orchards entered from

1 F. Köcher, *Keilschrifttexte zur assyrisch-babylonischen Drogen- und Pflanzenkunde* (1955).
2 R. D. Barnett, *Sculptures from the North Palace of Ashurbanipal at Niniveh* (1976), pl. xxiii.
3 L. M. Gallery, "The Garden of Egypt", in D. Schmandt-Besserat, *Immortal Egypt* (1978), pp. 43–49.
4 D. D. Luckenbill, *The Annals of Sennacherib* (1924), p. 97, l. 87.
5 ibid. p. 116 viii 64.
6 ibid. pp. 115–116 viii 47–73.
7 Contra *JNES* 24 (1965), p. 33.

the palace near the quay-wall. These extended as far as the *akītu*-house outside the city upstream.[8]

At Kalhu (Nimrud) c. 876 B.C. Aššur-nāṣir-apli II records the planting of royal gardens near the citadel and the R. Tigris which were watered by the Patinuhši-canal leading from the R. Zab (Plate V). Here he too planted trees, cuttings, saplings and seeds collected during his travels in many lands and hill countries. He lists 41 species of which the following can be identified with some certainty: cedar, cyprus, box, juniper *oxycecedrus* and *dupracea*, myrtle, date-palms, ebony, mulberry, olive, tamarisk, oak, terebinth, laurel, fir, willow, pomegranate, plum, loquat, pear, quince, medlar, fig, grape-vine and, less certainly, swamp-apple, *ricinus*, Persian lilac, walnut and various nut-bearing trees and aromatics. The effect was that "canal-water came flowing down from above through the gardens; the paths are full of scent; the waterfalls (sparkle) like the stars of heaven in the garden of pleasure. The pomegranate trees, which are clothed with clusters of fruit like vines, enrich the breezes in this garden of delight. I Aššur-nāṣir-apli gather fruit continuously in the garden of joys like a squirrel(?)".[9] These, and other public gardens were provided with cuttings and seeds from the palace holdings; as many as 1,200 saplings including 350 pomegranate, 400 fig and 450 medlar are noted in a single issue.[10]

The beauty of such palace gardens was noted by Sargon II during his campaign to Ulhu, the capital of Ursa in Urartu in 714 B.C. "the gardens", he records, "were the pleasant feature of the city and the trees were loaded with fruits and bunches of grapes".[11] The latter may be a reference to the common practice of training the grape-vine to run between adjacent trees. At Jerusalem there are references to the King's Garden similarly situated by the citadel with access through a gate between the double defence walls.[12] It was sufficiently private to have been used as a means of clandestine escape during a time of siege. It has been suggested that the gardens were watered from spillways from the Silwan tunnel system which irrigated the slopes of the Kidron valley.[13]

In the light of these examples it is reasonable to suppose that the gardens planted by Nebuchadnezzar II in Babylon c. 605 B.C. followed a similar tradition and on this basis the location of the so-called "Hanging Gardens of Babylon", said by Strabo in his description of The Seven World Wonders to be by the R. Euphrates (Plate VI *a*), can be reassessed. Since Koldewey's excavations in 1913

8 ABL 427.

9 *Iraq* XIV (1952), p. 33 ll. 38–48; CTN II (1973), pp. 239–240 ll. 48–52.

10 CTN II (1973), pp. 157–158, Nos. 139–140; p. 197 No. 198 (gives age and size).

11 TCL 3 233.

12 2 Kings 25:4; Jer. 39:4; 52:7.

13 *Biblical Archaeologist* 42 (1979), pp. 168–170.

the "Vaulted Building" (41×40 m.) located in the north-east of the Southern Palace complex adjoining the Procession Street and near the Ishtar Gate has been identified with the foundations of such gardens (Plates VI *b*–VII *a*). However, the 36 room complex of arched store-rooms has now been shown to have had other uses including palace stores and treasury and support for the raised Procession Street. The architecture is similar to buildings in Mari, Dūr-Kurigalzu and Eridu and the walls are not substantial enough to support a raised garden.[14] Such a location would mean that access from the royal apartments would have to be through public courtyards and administrative courtyards. Privacy, view and availability of water for irrigation are lacking.

I have therefore proposed that the site of the gardens should be sought on, and to the north of, the massive (110×230 m.) "Western Outwork" building between the Western palace, known to have been occupied by Nebuchadnezzar and his queen, and the R. Euphrates.[15] Dr. Mu'ayyad Damerji has independently suggested that the two 25 m. thick walls by the river may have been stepped and covered with bitumen and matting to form terraces.[16] Since Nebuchadnezzar says that he made this building (*halṣi rabīti*) 'like a mountain' it accords well with the classical traditions best exemplified by Berossus in his *Babyloniaca* and interpreted by Josephus: "At his palace he had knolls made of stone which he shaped like mountains and planted with all kinds of trees. Furthermore, he had a so-called "hanging-garden" (*pensile paradise*) planted because his wife, who came from Media, longed for such, which was the custom in her homeland".[17] This information, perhaps taken from Cleitarchus of Alexandra's history of Alexander and Ctesias, could well have been originally derived from Alexander's own observations in Babylon.[18] Excavations on the "Western Outwork" revealed the lower levels of a small palace-like building which could have been a 'summer-house, pavilion or kiosk' (*bītānu*) but without any entrance which must therefore have been at an upper level by raised way or bridge direct from the palace platform. Traces of this remain.

That these gardens were confined to terraces on the East bank of the Euphrates is unlikely in that they would have been exposed to the westerly desert winds and have had no privacy. It is probable that they were continued on terraces to the north protected by walls and formed an amphitheatre like layout visible from the

14 Cf. *Sumer* 35 (1979), pp. 134–136.

15 D. J. Wiseman, *An. St.* 33 (1983), pp. 140–141. *Nebuchadrezzar and Babylon* (British Academy Schweich Lectures 1983) forthcoming.

16 *Sumer* 37 (1981), pp. 56–81.

17 F. Josephus, *Contra Apionem* I 19; *Antiq. Jud.* X 11.

18 S. M. Burstein, *The babyloniaca of Berossus*, (1978), p. 27, n. 106.

palace itself (Plate VII *b*).[19] This would have the advantage of ready access also to extended gardens which may have reached as far as the *bīt akīti* temple and gardens which lay to the north outside the citadel (Plates VIII *a-b*). Nebuchadnezzar claims to have built a structure on superimposed terraces (*gigunâtim*) when extending his palace across the earlier double defence walls of the original 'Southern Citadel' to what is sometimes designated the Northern Palace. Here there were found deep drains suitable also for extensive irrigation. They connected with the *Östliche Ausfallvorwerk* which Bergamini has suggested to be a reservoir to ensure the movement of water throughout the extra-mural moat system rather than a bastion.[20]

The 'small palace' *bītānu* was a feature of Sennacherib's royal garden and Esarhaddon claims to have built his on a grander scale (48×16 m.) than any earlier king and to have surrounded it with gardens. There is no certainty that such garden buildings were evidence of western (Syrian) influence with their pillared porticos (*bīt-hilāni*?) or that they mark the change from strictly botanical to ornamental gardens as Oppenheim thought.[21]

The tradition of royal gardens can be traced back to the Old Kingdom in Egypt and in Babylonia alone to the reign of Adad-šuma-uṣur (c. 1200 B.C.) though letters from Mari mention royal gardens there and the practice was probably widespread throughout the ancient Near East by the third millennium. Nabû-apla-iddina mentions a garden in the inner quarter of Babylon (*ālu eššu*) c. 860 B.C. By that time gardens laid out by high officials are known from Egypt and only a dearth of similar information from cuneiform sources prevents our knowledge of their more common use by wealthy citizens elsewhere. The frequent reference to gardens or orchards in legal texts might support this.

Temple gardens

The ideal architectural layout of a building associated with a garden is attested from the Old Kingdom onwards in Egypt. In Sumer temple gardens are mentioned in epics and religious texts. Of the god Enki's garden it is said that "in its pleasant arbours the trees bear rich fruits, the birds nest, the giant carp plays among the 'honey plant', the marsh carp displays its tail for him among the young reeds. When Enki rises the fish rise before him against the waves".[22] The distinction between royal and ritual occassions in a garden is not easy to make. Since the queen is present with Ashurbanipal in the garden feasting it may indicate a festive rather than the religious situation often supposed. The *bitānu* was used as summer quarters and contained an inner area with sleeping quarters. That at Babylon, as

19 *An. St.* 33 (1983), p. 141.

20 *Mesopotamia* 12 (1977), pp. 136–139.

21 *JNES* 24 (1965), p. 331.

22 Al-Fouadi, *Enki's Journey to Nippur: The Journey of the Gods* (1969), p. 51, ll. 76–80.

IV b: Royal gardens depicted on bas-relief from the Palace of Ashurbanipal at Nineveh (British Museum 1/24730).

V: Description of the royal garden on the stela of Aššur-nāṣir-apli II at Kalhu (Nimrud, 876 B.C.).

VI a: Vegetation on the bank of the R. Euphrates at Babylon.

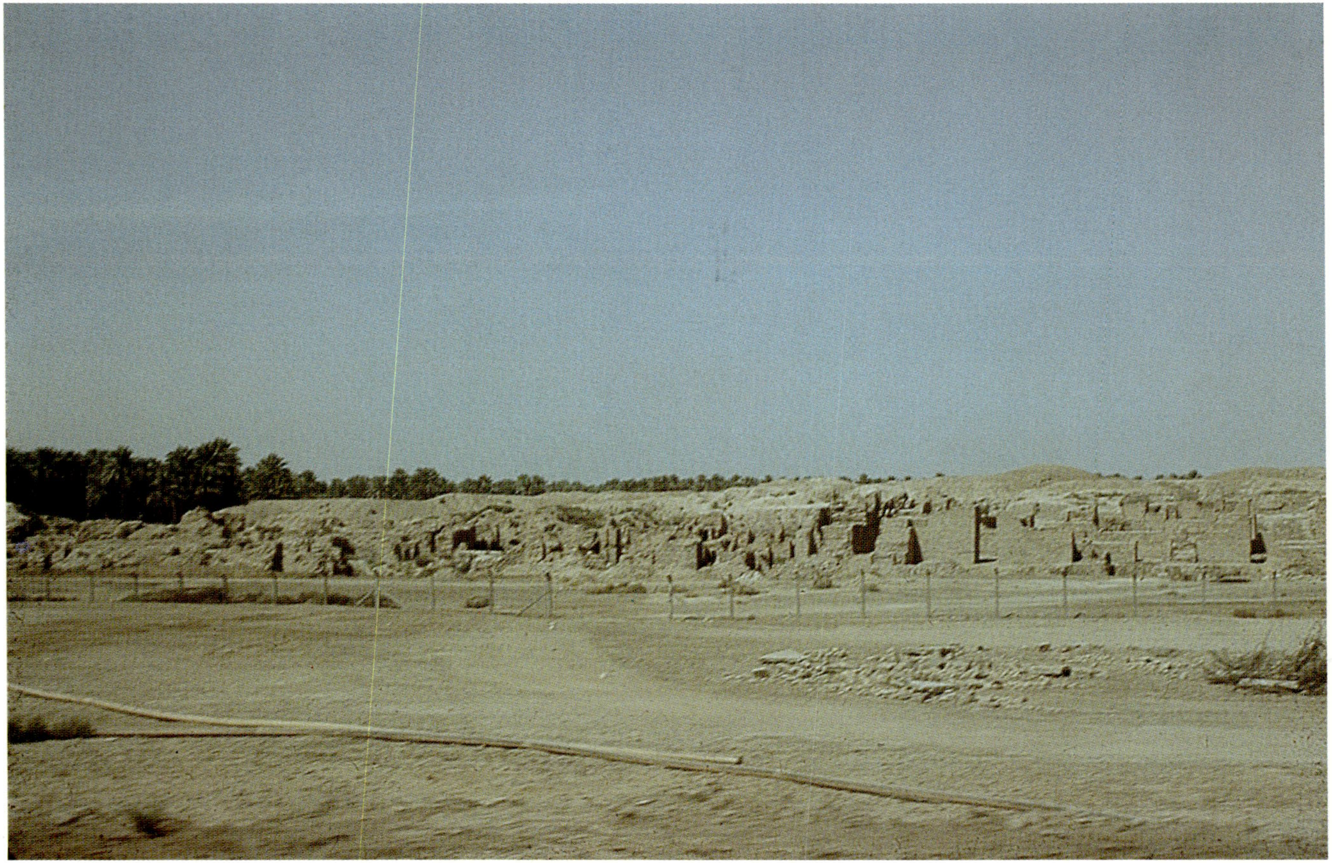

VI b: Excavations at Babylon, looking north-west across the Southern Citadel (1979).

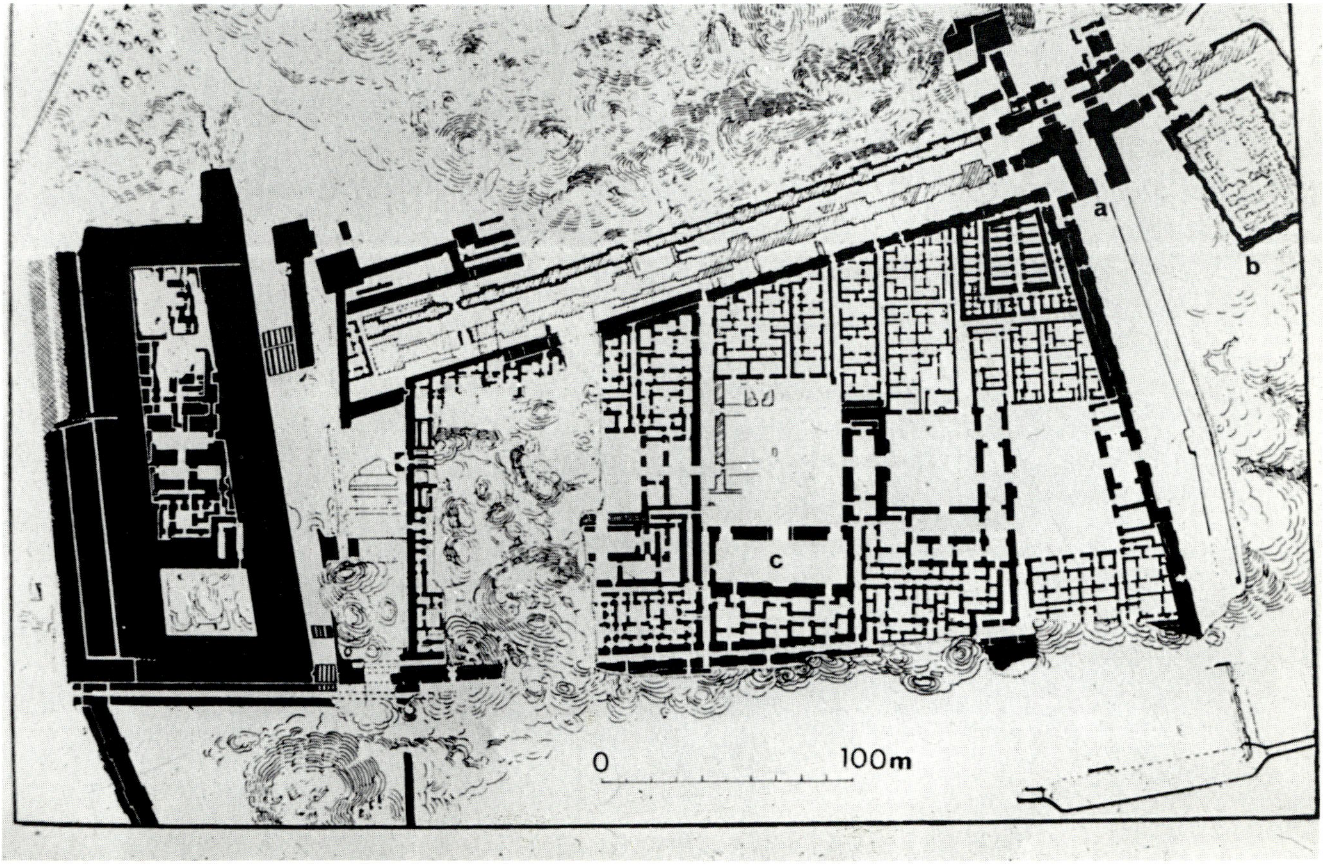

VII a: Plan of the Southern Citadel (after Koldewey).

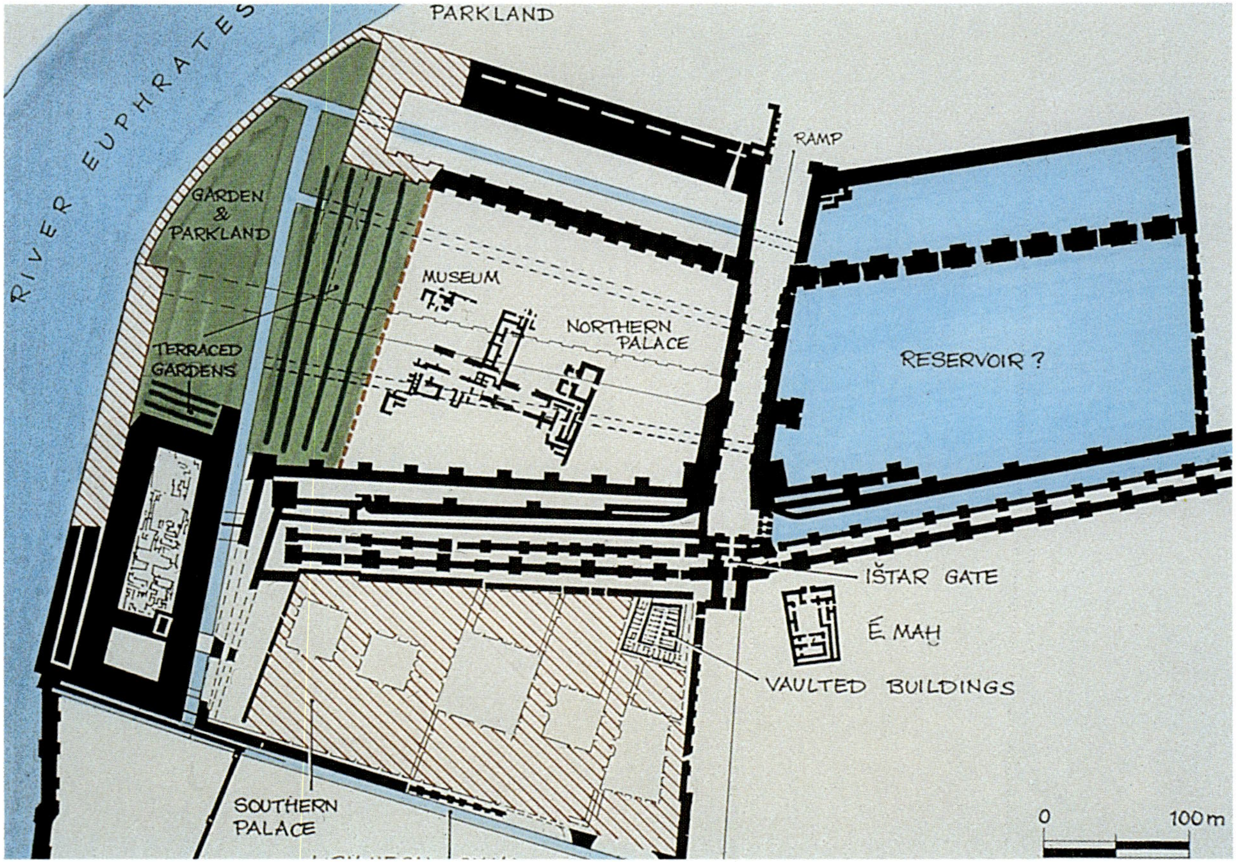

VII b: Reconstruction of the proposed location for the Royal ("Hanging") Gardens at Babylon.

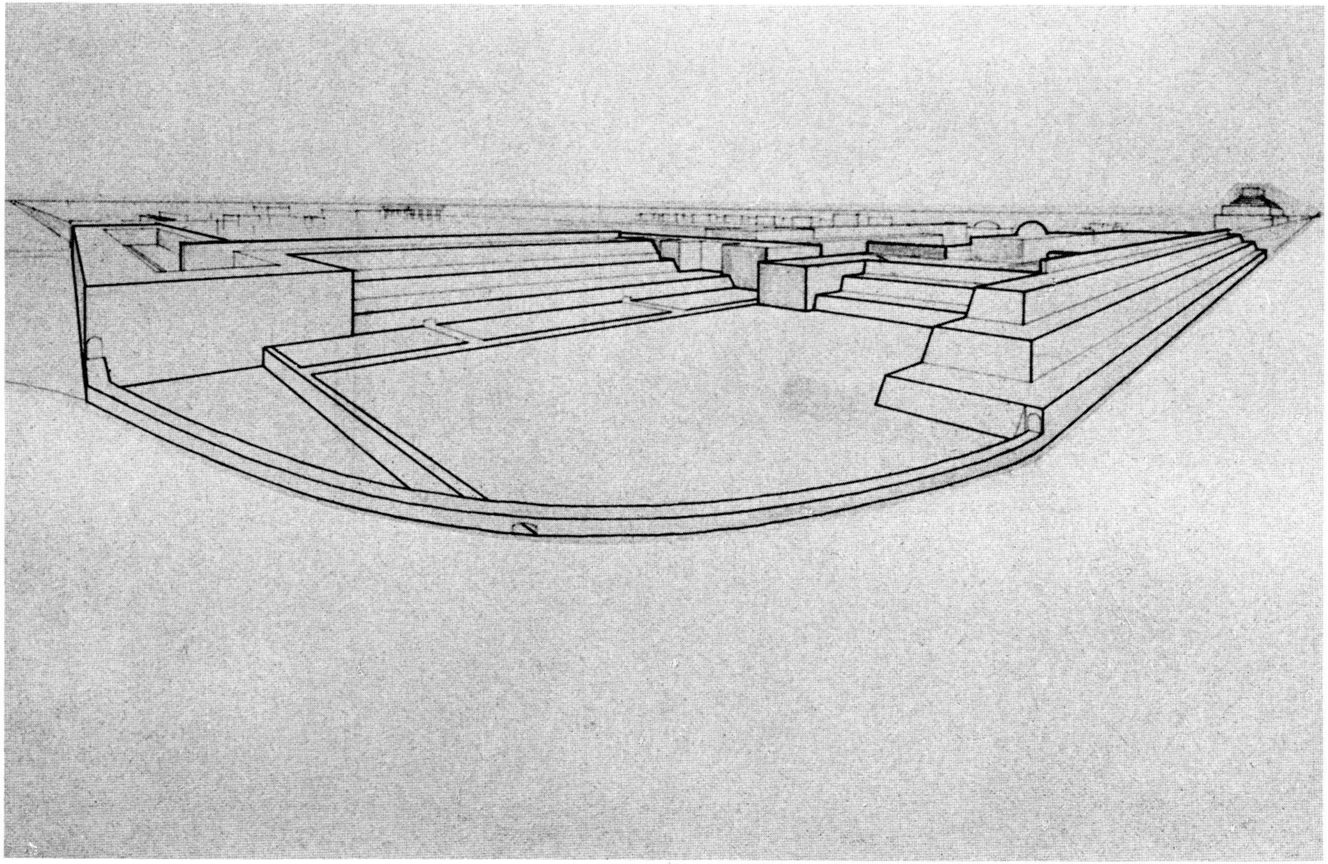

VIII a: Schematic basis for the reconstruction of the amphitheatre-type gardens at Babylon.

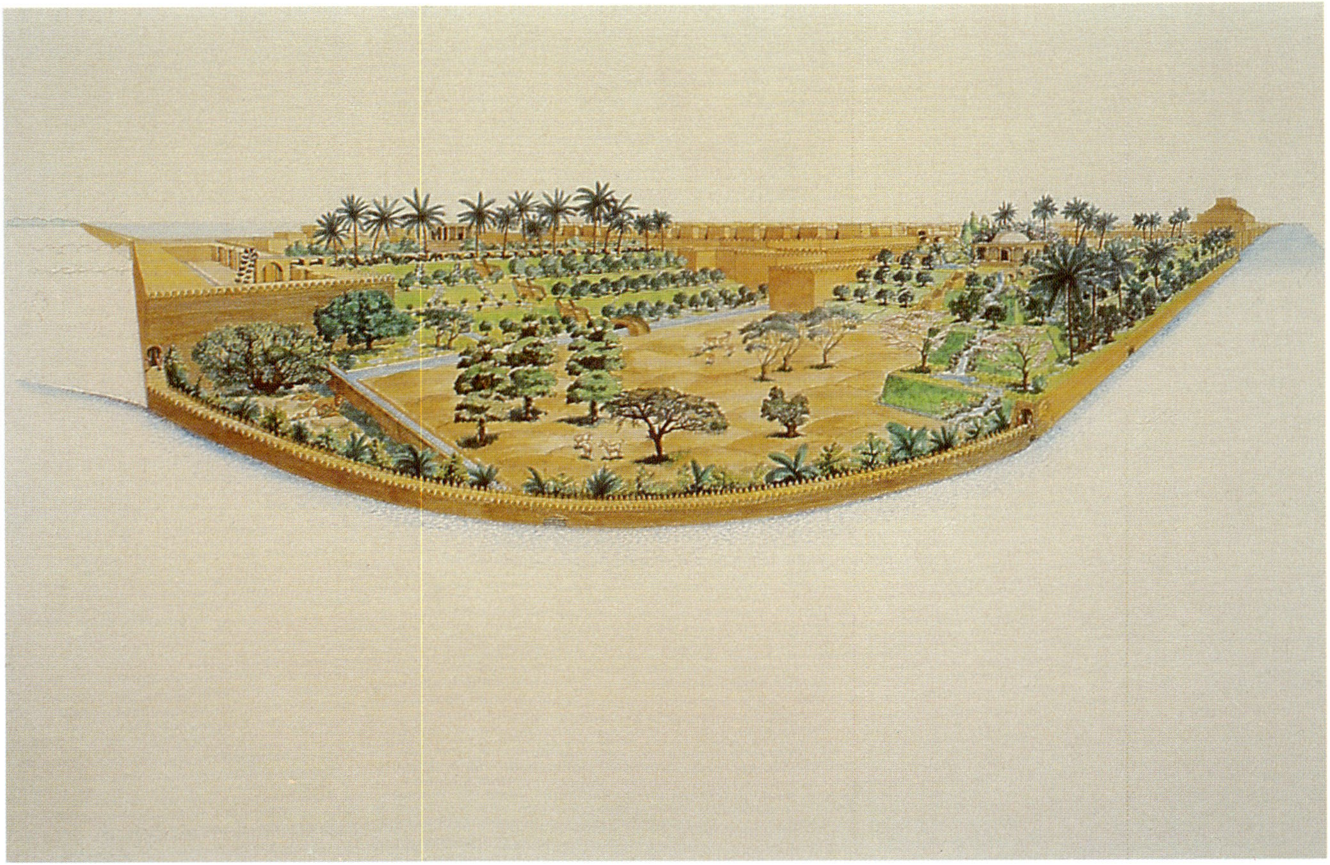

VIII b: Drawing of the proposed Royal Gardens of Babylon (Keith Talbott).

at Susa, was used for ritual purposes also. At Jerusalem Solomon said "I built houses for myself and planted vineyards. I made gardens and parks and planted all kinds of fruit in them. I made reservoirs to water groves of flowering trees." (Eccles. 2:4–6). The same gardens are traditionally those referred to in the *Song of Solomon* which has been considered a collection of cultic love songs full of references to the royal garden. In ancient Israel the association of groves of trees, exotic plants and the pagan rites enacted there led to the condemnation of such gardens by the prophets (e.g. Isaiah 1:29; 65:2–5; 66:17). Similar views may lie behind the deprecatory note by the Deuteronomist historian about the burial of godless kings such as Manasseh in his garden rather than in the ancestral royal sepulchre (2 Kings 21:18).

There are textual references, among others, to the temple garden of Innana to which she is said to have taken the *huluppu*-tree.[23] The practice of transporting large trees is shown on an Egyptian relief from Deir al-Bahari (c. 1500 B.C.) where the plant is shown with its root-ball protected by a basket aboard ship. In this way the god Khem, the god of gardens and regeneration is represented by actual plants and by their representation in architectural motifs. In Syria the gardens of Reshef and of El are mentioned and may be the origin of the gardens of Adonis.[24] In Assyria and Babylonia gardens are especially noted with the temples of Enlil, Anu, Adad and Nabû and the deities stated to go into their gardens, as did Nana into that at Ehuršaba in Babylon.[25] The purpose of such visits is not clear, being either for participation in some ritual, including the swearing of solemn oaths in their presence, or in out of doors living enjoyed by priest and layity alike. The principal ceremony at which the gods gathered was that of the New Year Festival in which a key part of the rites were performed in the *akītu*-temple which served as a pavilion amid a well kept garden, itself perhaps maintained as a symbol of fecundity.

The use of gardens. Ancient gardens in the Near East followed no stylised layout beyond terracing, but the larger gardens were subdivided into arboreum and orchard, flower and vegetable plots. For practical purposes in Babylonia this arrangement was classified as land plot requiring annual cultivation (*eqlum*) and perennial plantation (giš.kiri$_{11}$). The plants chosen were appropriate for each purpose. Since city palace and temple gardens were also developed as a pleasant feature of the capital city, as noted by Sennacherib and Sargon, the layout was such that 'the gardens enhance the pride of the city' according to a hymn to Ezida.

23 A. Shafer, *Sumerian Sources of Tablet XII of the Epic of Gilgamesh* (Univ. Pennsylvania Ph. D. 1963), l. 35, p. 30, n. 1.

24 UT 1088:3; *Ugaritica* VII (1968), pp. 10, 20, 26.

25 SBH 145 ii 24 cf. p. 22.

These gardens formed well-known landmarks in Babylonia[26] as in ancient Jerusalem.[27] Thus the appearance, form, foliage, blossom and fruit of the trees planted was important for the shade and fragrance they provided. Apart from the common date-palm, with its many uses, the tamarisk, sycomore and willow set in groves was where the owner could walk in the cool of the evening and entertain guests (cf. Genesis 3:8). The terebinth, laurel and acacia are also found as well as some evidence for the importation of the cedar, Easter Savin (*Juniperus excelsa*) and ebony.

The fruit orchard also was walled with a lockable gateway to protect against unnecessary incursions of thieves, animals, winds and sand. Here the commonest trees were the olive, almond, citron and apple and pomegranate. Many varities of nut-bearing trees and shrubs are attested in the texts especially the pistachio family. The *Persea gratis-ma* or avocado, carob (*ceratonia siliqua*) and walnut may be identified. Trees near rivers and marshes include the Euphrates Poplar, various willows (*salix alba*), oleander, reeds, rushes and papyrus in profusion.

Flowers are certainly known from pictorial respresentation, notably from Egypt, where the lotus, anemone and chrysanthemum was at home and from which they were sometimes exported. They were used for decorative purposes, personal greeting gifts to guests and as garlands. The identification of the rose in Babylonia (*amurdinnu*) is doubtful being based on etymology only. It is more likely to have been the blackberry or bramble to judge from historical texts where it is said to grow wild in the hills and to be thorny. As with more than five hundred plants named in texts and mostly referred to in medical texts and recipes more research is needed before classification.

One of the lists of plants copied by later scribes was that of 67 varieties of plants grown in the gardens of Marduk-apla-iddina II.[28] These were grouped into fifteen sections with vegetables predominating: onions, garlic, leeks, section of cress and lettuce; pulses: lentils, chickpeas and broad-beans; another of gourds presumably the watermelon, muskmelon and perhaps the bottle-gourd. Condiments – mint, majoram, coriander, cummin and dill occur in more than a single section. Other vegetables tentatively identified include alkaline plants and cress, truffles, rue, origanum and thyme and, in a separate section – turnips and radishes. Such palace gardens supplied vegetables to the palace by the basketful, while from outside the city in villages near rivers and canals vegetable gardens (*kirî ša urqi*) supplied the public market. Some gardens were clustered round a single settlement and one was called "Gardeners' Village".[29] Temple gardens provided basic ritual offerings

26 *ZA* 53 (1959) 238:4; BIN 1 70:14 (N. Bab. letter).

27 2 Kings 25:4; Eccles. 2:4–6; Neh. 3:15.

28 BM 466226; CT XIV 50; *ZA* 6 (1891), pp. 289–298.

29 ADD 778:8.

supplemented by the donations of worshippers, while some of the more exotic fruits may have been part of the royal gifts for temple maintenance.

Gardeners. The profession of gardener (*nukaribbu*) is mentioned in texts of all periods from Babylonia as it is in Egypt where the god of gardens, Khem, is represented by the 'tree' used as his symbol and hieroglyph. Gardeners were mostly employees, but occur as landowners and one Enlil-bāni was made a substitute king (*šar puhi*) during a time of national danger foretold by omens. However, when the evil passed he refused to vacate the throne of Babylon for its rightful owner Irra-immiti to resume office.[30] Records of payments and of work done indicate that status varied though most gardeners worked for the state or large private landowners. To judge from legal decisions made by the king Hammurapi (LH §§ 60–61, 64–65) a gardener who failed to lay out a plot as an orchard and produce fruit-bearing trees in it within four years and another who neglected the pollination of a date-palm orchard thus reducing its value were punished. Some gardeners specialised in fruitfarming or vegetables.[31] Female gardeners (*nukaribbatu*) and blind gardeners are cited.[32] A named Judean gardener was held among captives in Babylon and received royal rations in 592 B.C. indicating that he had some special expertise.[33]

In offering this paper as a contribution to our understanding of monarchies and socio-religious traditions in the ancient Near East it will be remembered that it was that region which first records the religious significance of gardens, as of trees in life and in the life after death. There too special gardens were associated with mountains (and possibly pyramids) and highlight the ancients' love of nature and reverence for beauty and fertility.

Selected Bibliography

M. S. Damerji, "Where are the Hanging Gardens?", *Sumer* XXXVII (1981), pp. 56–61 (Arabic).

E. Ebeling, "Garten", *Reallexikon der Assyriologie* III (1957–71), pp. 147–150.

L. M. Gallery, "The Garden of Ancient Egypt", in D. Schmandt-Besserat, *Immortal Egypt* (1978), pp. 43–49.

W. Nagel, "Where are the "Hanging Gardens" located in Babylon?", *Sumer* XXXV (1979), pp. 241–242.

A. L. Oppenheim, "On Royal Gardens in Mesopotamia", *Journal of Near Eastern Studies* 24 (1965), pp. 328–333.

D. J. Wiseman, "Mesopotamian Gardens", *Anatolian Studies* XXXIII (1983), pp. 137–144.

30 A. K. Grayson, *Assyrian and Babylonian Chronicles* (1975), p. 155, ll. 31–36.

31 C. Zaccagnini, *The Rural Landscape of the Land of Arrapḫe* (1979), pp. 127–128.

32 *YOS* 13 144:2; *UET* 5 494:18; I. J. Gelb, *St. Or* 46 (1976), p. 69.

33 E. F. Weidner, *Mélanges Syriens offerts à M. Réné Dussaud II* (1939), pp. 923–935.

Karol Myśliwiec (Polish Academy of Sciences, Warsaw)

ICONOGRAPHIC, LITERARY AND POLITICAL ASPECTS OF AN ANCIENT EGYPTIAN GOD'S IDENTIFICATION WITH THE MONARCH

Ancient Egyptian kings were associated with various gods. Both the official royal titulary and the iconography of each pharaoh reveal a general tendency to show the monarch as a picture of the god. There existed some obvious identifications, e.g. with the god Horus, considered to be the predecessor of all Egyptian kings. According to Egyptian beliefs, the pharaoh was the incarnation of the sun god Re during his lifetime, and was posthumously identified with Osiris, the god of the dead.

One particular form of the solar deity was in many respects considered a double of the king. This was the god Atum, the chief divinity in the local pantheon of Heliopolis, the primeval god who created himself and the whole universe, a form of the sun attributed particularly to the sunset. The earliest literary record pointing to the king's identity with Atum occurs in the chapter 135 (spell 213) of the "Pyramid Texts" which are the oldest known manual of Egyptian theology:

"Thy (i.e. the king's) arm is that of Atum,
Thy shoulders are those of Atum,
Thy belly is that of Atum,
Thy back is that of Atum,
Thy bottom is that of Atum,
Thy two legs are those of Atum,
Thy face is that of Anubis"[1].

Remarkable is the fact that among the seven parts of the king's body which are enumerated in this spell, six are referred to Atum, and only one to another god.

While the origin of these special affiliations remains unknown, the iconography of Atum reveals several features which exemplify the permanency of this god's identification with the pharaoh during more than three thousand years, i.e. from the Old Kingdom to the Roman Period. In his anthropomorphic version, Atum is usually depicted as a man wearing a short apron, a broad collar[2] and the double crown of Lower and Upper Egypt. This crown, which symbolizes the unification

1 Translation of A. Piankoff, The Pyramid of Unas, Bollingen Series 40, 5 (1968), p. 59.

2 On the king's assimilation with Atum in respect to this detail of their attire, cf. Papyrus Brooklyn 47.218.50, III, 3: "Pharaon V.P.S. ... donne son collier "wsḫ" à Atoum". Translation of. J.-C.

of both parts of the country, is also a characteristic detail of the royal attire. Even in the case of the numerous bronze statuettes showing Atum as an eel with the shield of cobra, the figure's anthropomorphic head often wears the royal double crown[3].

The only significant iconographic difference between the pharaoh and the Heliopolitan god consists in the shape of the beard. The god's beard is bent forwards at the lower end, whereas the pharaoh's artificial beard appears cut straight in its lower part. Atum was thus the only Egyptian god, whose identification with the monarch was permanently emphasized by his physical appearance.

Another record of this association may be found in Egyptian representations of the coronation ceremony. This historical moment was often depicted as a scene concentrating around the tree "ished". The king, appearing between the branches of the tree, is usually represented here as being crowned by one god, whereas his names are being recorded by another deity. Atum often appears in one of these two important parts: he is either crowning the pharaoh or writing down his names[4]. His presence in this case is more or less obvious, for the described ceremony most probably originates from Heliopolis.

The most popular iconographic version of the coronation ceremony is provided by numerous sculptured scenes on walls of Egyptian temples and on objects of religious character, e.g. on the wooden panels from the royal throne found in the tomb of Tuthmosis IV[5]. These scenes often show only one god – usually the chief divinity of the local pantheon (e.g. Atum in Eastern Delta, Amon in Thebes)[6] – putting his hands on the crown of a kneeling king. An enlarged version of this scene also represents a goddess standing in front of the king and handing the symbol of life to him, whereas she is confirming the coronation by putting her other hand on the pharaoh's forehead. Several scenes in the chapel of Queen Hatshepsut in Karnak are built up according to this scheme[7]. The goddess who appears the most frequently in this context is Wert-hekau, "the great of magy"[8]. She is sometimes replaced in this function by Hathor, Mut, Wadjet of Ament[9].

Goyon, Confirmation du Pouvoir Royal au Nouvel An, *BdE*, LII (Le Caire 1972), p. 60, 93, note 88.

3 K. Myśliwiec, Aal oder Schlange? – Atum oder Meresger?, MDAIK 37, 1981, p. 377–382; Id., Quelques aspects de la zoomorphie du dieu Atoum, Africana Bulletin 31, 1983, p. 25–36; Id., Drei Bronzefiguren der ägyptischen Spätzeit, Studien zu Sprache und Religion Ägyptens (Fs. W. Westendorf), Göttingen, 1984, p. 809–817.

4 Id., Die Rolle des Atum in der išd-Baum-Szene, MDAIK 36, 1980, p. 349–356.

5 Porter and Moss, Bibliography, I^2, p. 561.

6 K. Myśliwiec, Le naos de Pithom, BIFAO 78, 1978, p. 194–195.

7 P. Lacau, H. Chevrier, Une chapelle d'Hatshepsout à Karnak, II, 1979, pl. 2, 3, 11.

8 E.c. Id., pl. 2, assise 7, 8, and pl. 11, four scenes.

9 Id. Ib., pl. 11.

Almost all of these goddesses could be identified or associated by ancient Egyptians with the protective cobra snake which usually decorates the forehead of Egyptian kings. These goddesses were also interpreted in Egypt as daughters of the sun god or as this god's eyes[10]. Therefore, even if Atum does not always occur as the divinity performing the coronation, his spiritual presence may be deduced from the participation of his daughters, i.e. daughters of the sun god.

On the other hand, in the series of conventional scenes belonging to the coronation cycle in Theban temple reliefs, Atum usually appears as one of two "acolytes" introducing the king to the chief divinity. The companion god is an Upper Egyptian divinity, most frequently Khonsu or Monthu.

Considering all known iconographic versions of the royal coronation, we may conclude that the "Lord of Heliopolis", almost constantly accompanying the monarch at this moment, must have been strictly associated with the very notion of kingship. The inscriptions accompanying scenes of coronation as well as those of the royal jubilee remain in accord with this role. Such formulae as "the years of Atum" or "the kingship of Atum" belong to the most frequent wishes addressed to the king on those occasions, and recorded in these inscriptions[11].

At this point, it would be almost impossible and futile to quote comprehensive literary evidence, but numerous allusions to the royal character of Atum and various mentions of the features that the pharaoh shares with the Heliopolitan god, abound in Egyptian texts of all kinds. A few examples would be sufficient to illustrate these concepts. A king of the Middle Kingdom is called "Atum himself"[12]; the text of a stela of Sebekhotep IV (Cairo JE 51911) describes the king as a "living protector of Atum"[13], Ramesses II is called the "living picture of your father Atum on earth"[14], the papyrus Chester Beatty IX, BM 10689, dated to the same rule, contains the following formula: "O Atum! Hail to thee, O Khopri ... thou placest thine arms around the king, lord of the Two Lands ... and causest that his 'ka' may be flourishing there for eternity"[15]. A text of the Roman Period in the temple of Esna refers to an

10 K. Myśliwiec, La mère, la femme, la fille et la variante féminine du dieu Atoum, *Et. Trav.*, XIII, 1983, p. 297–304.

11 Cf. e.c., ZÄS 82, 1957, p. 123 (nr. 16), 134 (nr. 5), 128 (nr. 6); comp. the association contained in the sentence: "Ich habe seinen Namen in Theben dauernd gemacht wie den Namen des Atum in Heliopolis", (Ibid., p. 135 nr. 6); see also examples in MDAIK 23, 1968, p. 134, pl. 35, b and 36, a; BIFAO 17, p. 29; ASAE 52, p. 102, and many other places.

12 King Amenemhet II, inscription in Beni Hassan (Rec. Trav., 1, p. 163).

13 Stela from Karnak (MDAIK 24, p. 195, 199).

14 Stela from Kuban, in the collection St Ferriol (RE, N.S., 1, 1919, p. 23).

15 A. H. Gardiner, *Hieratic Papyri in the British Museum.* Third Series, Chester Beatty Gift, London, 1935, p. 91.

emperor as to the "l'héritier parfait d'Atoum qui lui a transmis sa fonction, après lui avoir fait un acte de cession à son nom"[16].

The identification of the king with Atum in literary texts of Old, Middle and New Kingdom has been traced by Ph. Derchain[17]. Literary evidence from the Late Period has been studied by J.-C. Goyon based on the examples contained in the Brooklyn Papyrus 47.218.50, and concerning the ceremonies of the confirmation of royal authority at the New Year[18]. In this unique document the king is known by such epithets as "The Heliopolitan", "The Emissary (ỉpwty) of Atum", and "Atum in his manifestation" (Itm m b3.f)[19].

The most popular epithet of Atum, "nb Iwnw" = "The Lord of Heliopolis" undergoes a significant evolution in the course of the centuries. From a certain moment of Egyptian history onwards, perhaps since the beginning of the 18th Dynasty, and most probably since the rule of Queen Hatshepsut, this epithet occurs expanded to the form "Nb t3wy Iwnw" = "The Lord of the Two Lands (and) of Heliopolis". The element "Lord of the Two Lands" (i.e. Lower and Upper Egypt) has evidently been taken from the royal titulary, in which it often introduces the pharaoh's prenomen[20]. Why would some Egyptian theologians suddenly have felt the need to stress the Heliopolitan god's presence in both parts of Egypt at the beginning of the 18th Dynasty? Historical records are too scanty to give a definite explanation of this problem, but the development of Egyptian history up to the "Amarna Period" would suggest a hypothesis which is based on some trends in this period's political theology. The progressive development of solar cults in Thebes at the beginning of the 18th Dynasty, culminating in the so-called "Atenist heresy" of Amenophis IV, was a result of increasing influences of Helipolitan theology in Thebes, i.e. in a place which had for a long time been the domain of the powerful local god Amun[21]. As the beginning of the solar god's astonishing career in Thebes coincides with the dynastic unrest dating back to the time of Hatshepsut, we may conclude from these two facts that Heliopolis was enlarging its influence in Upper Egypt on the base of a political support granted

16 Esna text 332 bis, 28, published and translated by S. Sauneron, *Esna III*, Le Caire, 1968, p. 267, and Idem, *Esna V*, 1962, p. 228.

17 Ph. Derchain, Ménès, le roi "quelqu'un", *RdE* 18, 1966, p. 34; Id., La réception de Sinouhé à la cour de Sésostris I, RdE 22, 1970, p. 81–2; comp. G. A. Wainwright, Seshat and the Pharaoh, JEA 26, 1940, p. 34–35, 40; G. Röder in ASAE 52, p. 373.

18 J.-C. Goyon, op. cit., (cf. note 2).

19 Id. Ib., p. 16.

20 A. Gardiner, *Egyptian Grammar*, 3d ed., 1973, p. 74. On the evolution of this title concerning Atum, s. K. Myśliwiec, Studien zum Gott Atum, II, HÄB 8, Hildesheim 1979, p. 85–102, 112–114.

21 K. Myśliwiec, Amon, Atum and Aton. The evolution of Heliopolitan influences in Thebes, in: *L'Egyptologie en 1979. Axes priorotaires de recherches*, II, Paris, 1982, p. 285–289.

by its clergy to some royal dynastic ambitions, starting with those of Hatshepsut[22]. The competition between the local god and the intrusive Heliopolitan deity seems to have found an expression in the textual legend which usually accompanies the representations of Atum. Instead of being called simply "Lord of Heliopolis", for political reasons Atum became a "Lord of the Two Lands" as well. This label emphasized the expansion of Heliopolitan influences upon Upper Egypt. On the other hand, this epithet could have been interpreted as just a written version of the same royal feature that was iconographically illustrated by the god's double crown.

Other elements of the king's association with Atum may be deduced from the god's zoomorphic figures. The sphinx with royal head, a form of the sun god, labelled sometimes with the name "Atum"[23], was often depicted as treading foreign captives. In a similar context the anthropomorphic pharaoh appears on pylons of Egyptian temples, as well as in scenes decorating royal thrones and chariots[24].

Syncretistic forms and names of the solar deity encouraged a flexible distribution of their visual aspects between the principal elements of the solar cycle, which are: Khepre, Re-Harakhte and Atum. That is why Atum could also be associated with the scarab – an animal which was usually attributed to Khepre. An illustration of this particular case is the so-called "great scarab" in Karnak. Its socle is decorated with a stela representing the king Amenophis III kneeling in front of Atum. The god is shown as wearing the double crown. Even in this case the royal aspect of the Heliopolitan god has not been overlooked. The animal venerated as "herald" (wḥm) of Atum in Heliopolis was the bull. The same animal's figure constituted an old symbol of kingship in Egypt, which may be deduced from the epithet "Strong Bull" – one of the most frequent components of the pharaoh's "Horus name"[25].

A particular chapter in Ancient Egyptian political theology is connected with the representations of the sun god's nightly journey in the other world. Various illustrations of this concept occur on the walls of many tombs, particularly in Thebes, and on objects found in these tombs. During his travels through the nether-world the sun god usually appears as a ram-headed human being standing in a bark, and often accompanied by a snake and other gods. Although this divinity most frequently is labeled as "Iwf" = "The Flesh", and quite rarely as "Atum" or "Re", an explicit association with the "Lord of Heliopolis" is visible in

22 Id. Ib., p. 289.

23 Id., Studien zum Gott Atum I, HÄB 5, Hildesheim, 1978, pl. IV.

24 Id., XVIIIth Dynasty before the Amarna Period, fascicle XVI, 5 in the series "Iconography of Religions", Leiden (in press), pl. XIX–XXI.

25 A. H. Gardiner, Egyptian Grammar, 3[d] ed., 1973, p. 72.

1. The god Atum represented on a Late Period wooden coffin. Rijksmuseum van Oudheden te Leiden.
(Photo: Courtesy, Rijksmuseum van Oudheden)

2. Ram-headed Atum. Relief on an Early Ptolemaic stone sarcophagus. Egyptian Museum, Cairo, CG 29301.
(Photo: Andrzej Bodytko, Polish Center of Archaeology, Cairo)

3. Three divinities of the solar cycle: Re, Atum and Khepre. Relief on a Late Period stone sarcophagus. Egyptian Museum, Cairo, T.N. 3/3/21/1. *(Photo: Andrzej Bodytko)*

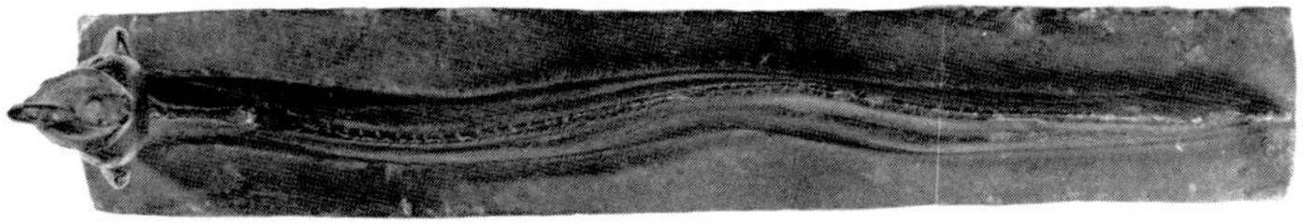

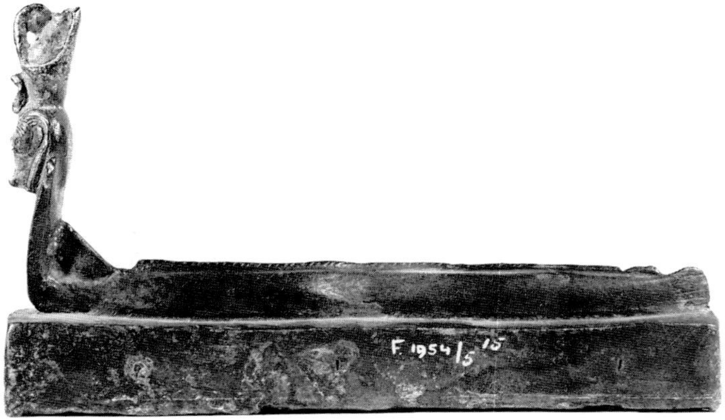

Bronze figurines representing Atum as an eel with the shield of cobra and with royal head:

1–2: Rijksmuseum van Oudheden te Leiden, no. F. 1954/5. 15. Dimensions: Length: 19,0 cm; Total height: 10,9 cm; Width of base: 3,3 cm.
(Photo: Courtesy, Rijksmuseum van Oudheden)

3–4: British Museum no. 36151. Dimensions: L. 30,0 cm; H. 14,4 cm. H. of the head with headdress: 7,5 cm.
(Photo: Courtesy, British Museum)

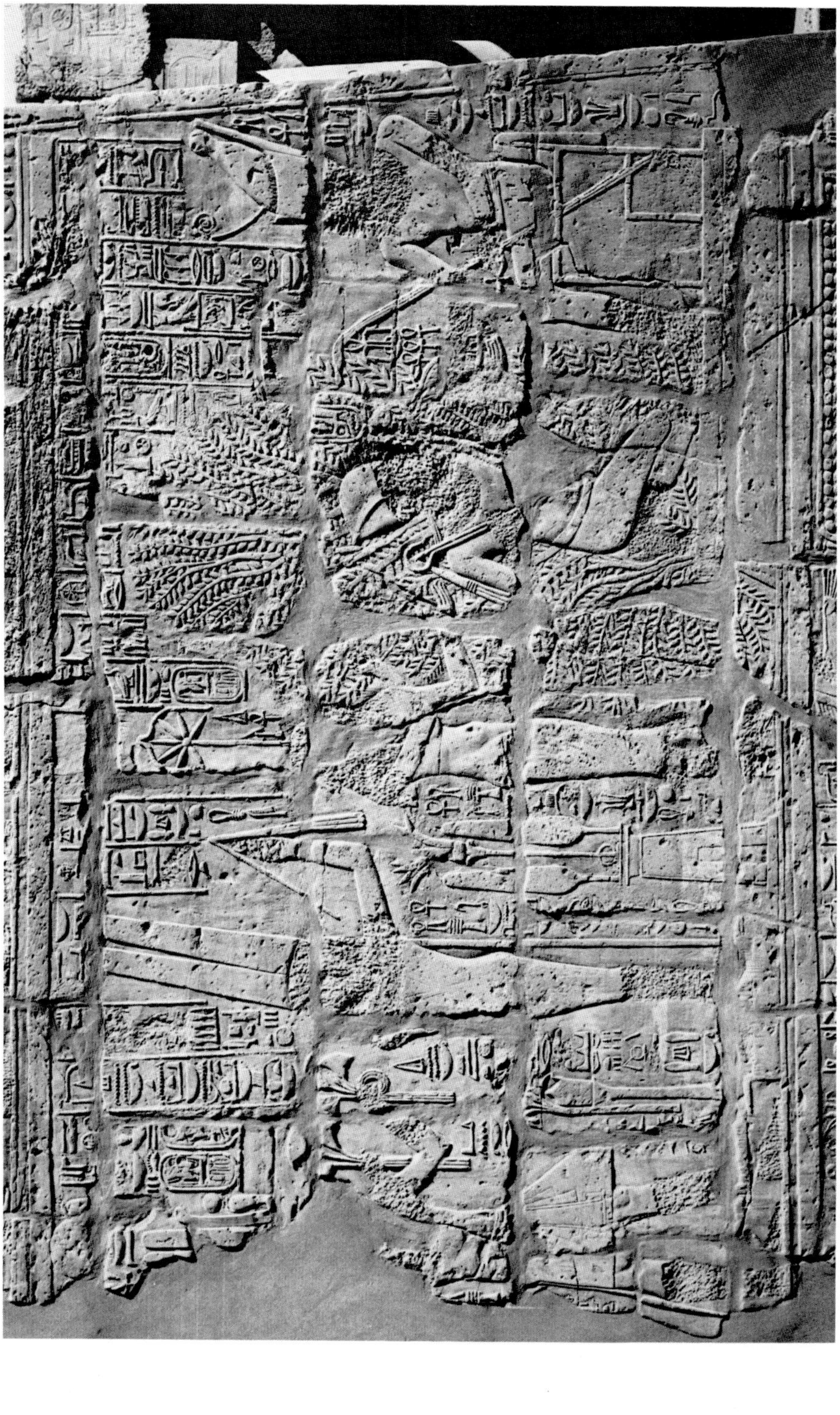

Scene with the tree "ished" on the 2[d] pylon of the Karnak temple. Ramses II kneeling in front of Atum.
(Photo: Zbigniew Doliński, Polish Center of Archaeology, Cairo)

Atum writing the names of king Takeloth III on the tree "ished". Relief in the temple of Osiris-Ruler-of-Eternity at Karnak.
(Photo: Dieter Johannes, German Archaeological Institute, Cairo)

The coronation of the king:

1. Hatshepsut crowned by Amun. Relief on an obelisk in Karnak.
   (Photo: Zbigniew Doliński)

2. Ramesses II crowned by Atum. Relief on the naos from Pithom. Egyptian Museum, Cairo.
   (Photo: Waldemar Jerke, Polish Center of Archaeology, Cairo)

Three versions of the coronation scene represented on walls of the chapel of Hatshepsut at Karnak. The goddesses standing in front of Hatshepsut are:

1. Mut
2. Ament
3. Hathor.

(Photo: Karol Myśliwiec)

1. Scenes of the coronation ceremony decorating the mortuary temple of Ramesses II (Ramesseum). *(Photo: Karol Myśliwiec)*

2. Ramesses IV receiving the signs of life and introduced by the gods Monthu and Atum. Relief in the temple of Khonsu at Karnak. *(Photo: Zbigniew Doliński)*

The name of Atum and his epithet "The Lord of the Two Lands /and/ of Heliopolis", as parts of the royal titulary:

2. The socle of a sphinx in the mortuary temple of king Sethos I at Qurna.
(Photo: Karol Myśliwiec)

1. Fragment of a column with names of king Horemheb. Egyptian Museum, Cairo, T.N. 10/12/14/7. *(Photo: Andrzej Bodytko)*

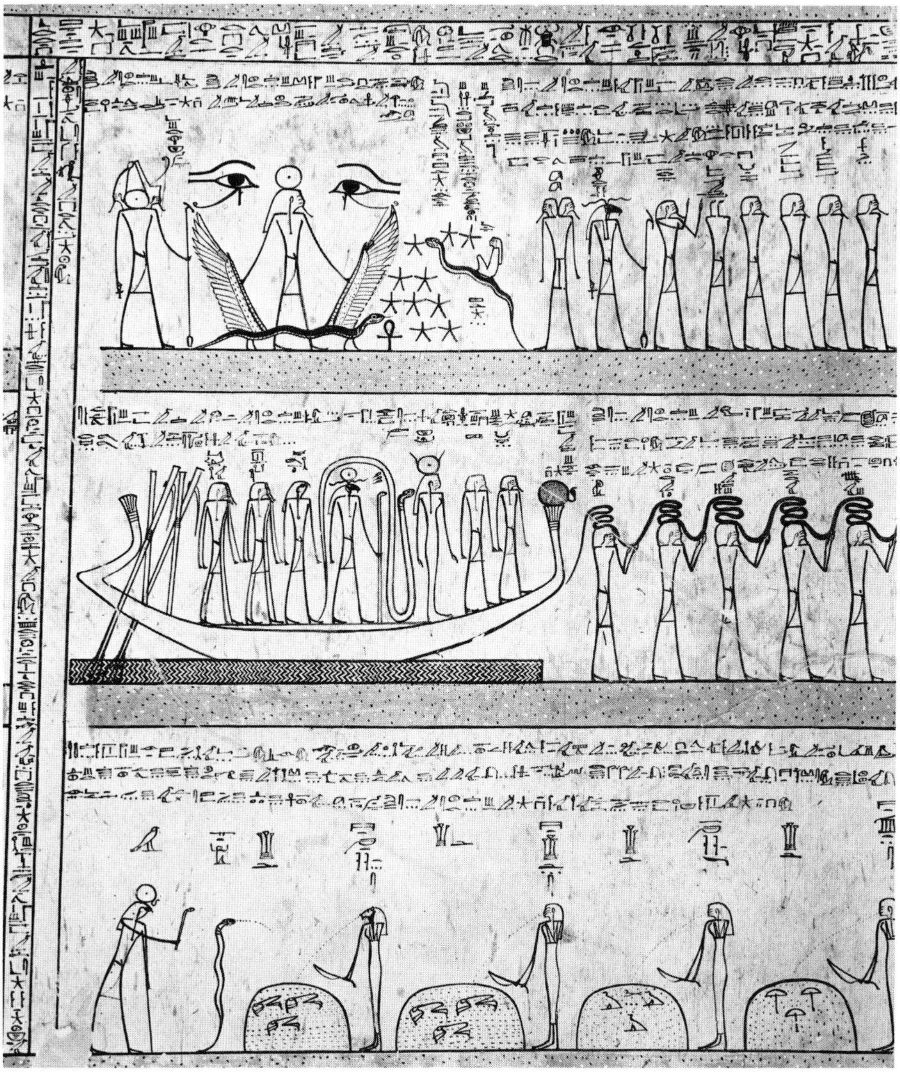

Scenes from the book "Amduat" depicted on walls of the tomb of Tuthmosis III:
upper register: Atum as solar deity appearing between the wings of a snake:
middle register: the ram-headed god "Flesh" in his bark. *(Photo: Zbigniew Doliński)*

1. Atum wearing a long head-cloth with a sun disc. Relief on a funerary monument. Egyptian Museum, Cairo, JE 89624. *(Photo: Waldemar Jerke)*

2. Basalt statue of god Atum, found in Herculanum. *(Photo: Courtesy Dr. Fulvio Da Salvia)*

those cases, in which "Iwf" is shown with human head wearing the royal double crown.

After the New Kingdom, the syncretistic form of the solar divinity Re-Harakhte-Atum-Khepre increases in popularity. In scenes decorating monuments of funerary character this god occurs as an anthropomorphic figure in the attitude of Osiris wearing a crown which is composed of two feathers. A similar headdress adorns the king's head in numerous scenes of religious character, not only in monuments related to the other world, but also in other sanctuaries, e.g. in temples connected with the royal jubilee ("heb-sed" – temples). This coincidence may be interpreted as a feature which relates the king to the nightly form of the sun god, Atum being one of this god's components.

The same syncretistic solar divinity is sometimes represented as wearing a long head-cloth with a sun disc above it. This picture may illustrate the concept of the king's being a "Son of Re", for this epithet usually occurs as the title introducing the "nomen" in the titulary of every pharaoh[26]. Atum even occurs, particularly on monuments of funerary character, as a similar figure without the solar disc on his head[27]. It may appear as a great surprise that the only large size stone statue of this god known until now has the same iconographic features as this figure[28]. Found in Herculanum, and originating from the Heliopolitan-Memphite region, this black basalt statue (height: 90 cm) raises the question, why the statuary of the Heliopolitan god, who was one of the most important personalities in Ancient Egyptian religion, remains almost unknown until now. Although none of the great temples in Lower Egypt, where the worship of Atum must have been particularly frequent, has remained up to the present time, we could expect some of the god's stone statues to have been transferred from these temples to Alexandria or to Rome during the Greco-Roman period. Since "The Lord of Heliopolis" is so far represented by only one statue of important size, we may propose the following hypothesis:

The iconography of Atum being either a copy or an illustration of the king's features, it is possible that also – vice versa – the royal statuary, and particularly the statues showing the monarch with the double crown or with a head-cloth, could be considered as symbolic pictures of the Heliopolitan god. If this presumption proves true, we may have justified reasons to believe that statues of Atum himself not only are rare, but were also rare in Ancient Egypt. Royal statuary would have represented both the monarch and the Heliopolitan god.

The particular similarity of the pharaoh with the "Lord of Heliopolis" was doubtless qualifying the latter as an easy instrument of political theology and

26 Id. Ib., p. 74.

27 K. Myśliwiec, Studien zum Gott Atum II (cf. note 20), pl. VII.

28 Id. Ib., catalogue nr. 24, pl. XIII–XVI.

dynastic policy. In the present state of our knowledge we have just been able to outline this problem on the example of one historical episode which was the "Amarna Period" of Akhenaten. Let us hope that future discoveries will throw some new light on the mutual influences of theological and political aspects of Ancient Egyptian religion.

Jean Leclant (Académie des Inscriptions et Belles-Lettres, Paris)

RECENT RESEARCHES IN THE PYRAMIDS WITH TEXTS AT SAQQARAH

If the great step pyramid of Djoser, the famous king of the IIIrd dynasty (c. 2650 B.C.) at Saqqarah, and the three famous pyramids of Giza, Kheops, Khephren and Mykerinos, Pharaohs of the IVth dynasty (c. 2550–2470 B.C.), are very well known, on the contrary, attention was less focused on the pyramids that are located south of Saqqarah, the ones of Ounas, the last Pharaoh of the Vth dynasty, of Teti, Pepi I, Merenre and Pepi II, Pharaohs of the VIth dynasty (c. 2350–2200 B.C.).

A century ago (more precisely during the last weeks of 1880), Gaston Maspero discovered them at Saqqarah-South; he had just arrived in Egypt and showed immediately that they were pyramids with texts: the walls of the corridors and the subterranean chambers of those pyramids in ruins are covered with inscribed columns presenting cartouches of those Pharaohs. Immediately, Gaston Maspero proceeded to the clearing in order to enter in those pyramids. He had ink-rubbings and a copy of the texts made of the remains of the walls that were still standing and accessible. The inner part of the pyramid of Ounas was almost intact, and it is still the only one that can be visited to this day. On the other hand, for the other pyramids, that were filled with stones and broken fragments while the enormous masses of beams and the walls were in a very unstable position; one must admire the intrepidity of Gaston Maspero and his assistants for their work and their success.

As early as 1882, with a brief description of the state of the area, G. Maspero published the texts in a series of articles compiled in the *Recueil de Travaux*, in a typographical composition and a translation. It was extremely audacious in fact and for that time a superb realization. As early as 1894, those articles were brought together into a volume. The exceptional value of the Texts of the Pyramids, the most ancient funerary composition of the world, focused immediately the attention of the scholars and the public. And for a century, they continue to constitute the most important comprehensive material for the study of Egyptian religion – and for the fundamental knowledge of the Pharaonic civilization. Comparable formulae being found on several pyramids, the German Kurt Sethe prepared in 1908 a synoptic edition which remains a classic work, with a division of the texts into chapters (*Spruch*), subdivided into paragraphs.

In the years 1925–1930, restarting the clearing of the Saqqarah-South sector, the Swiss Gustave Jéquier discovered around the pyramid of Pepi II, remains of funerary chambers containing texts, first of the queen Oudjebten, then of the queens Neit and Apouit, the wifes of Pepi II, and lastly the tomb of a petty king, unknown until then, dating from the beginning of the 1st Intermediate Period, Aba; he published them, giving additional texts.

As I have said, the interior of the pyramids of Teti, Pepi I and Merenre were full of stone fragments – and Gaston Maspero was only able to copy the texts on the visible walls. This was the reason why, in 1951, J. Sainte-Fare Garnot and J.-Ph. Lauer started a new series of researches on the pyramids with texts at Saqqarah, under the sponsorship of the National Center for the Scientific Research (CNRS) – Paris –, in collaboration with the Egyptian Service for Antiquities. Their first purpose was the clearing of the pyramid of Teti. Interrupted several times by the international situation, and then by the premature death of J. Sainte-Fare Garnot, the archeological work was continued by myself from 1963. After Teti, I proceeded with Pepi I and Merenre. It is this work and the results of twenty years of work that I would like to present here, focusing especially on the pyramidal complex of Pepi I.

In order to reach the inside of the pyramid of Pepi I, first the long slope which, from the North, gave access to the funerary rooms had to be cleared; then the remains of the pyramids right above the funerary chambers were removed in order to penetrate directly inside it. For that clearing which was really colossal and dangerous, one had to proceed in a miner-like manner, advancing among broken stones that were in a very unstable position, consolidated little by little, providing supports while progressing toward the inner part of the pyramid. The slabs placed in a 'chevron'-like pattern which covered the funerary chambers – very large stones of about 30 tonnes each – were also broken. Thousands and thousands of stones fragments were extracted, brought to the surface by a long chain of workers, from the bowels of the pyramid to our storage rooms. Among them, thousands of them bore inscriptions: they were inventoried, classified, copied (scale tracing and ⅕ reduced drawings), photographed and studied. The elements of the walls *in situ* were surveyed and reported carefully in details. The epigraphic study of this enormous material formed little by little large puzzles corresponding to each of the broken walls, i.e. the reconstitution of the texts on paper. How did these assemblages take shape? One must take into account all kinds of marks: the form of the stones, dimensions, the nature of the stone, the outline of the broken fragments, the color of the inscriptions, the disposition and also the meaning of the texts – for, if one must have some knowledge of architectural matters in order to execute the clearing and the support, one must also be a philologist and understand the meaning of those inscriptions.

I a: Saqqarah. Funerary Chambers of Pepi I. Pile of fallen stones.

Ib: Saqqarah. Pyramid of Pepi I. Stones being brought out of the funerary chambers by the workers.

II a: Saqqarah. Pyramid of Pepi I. Copying the texts *in situ*.

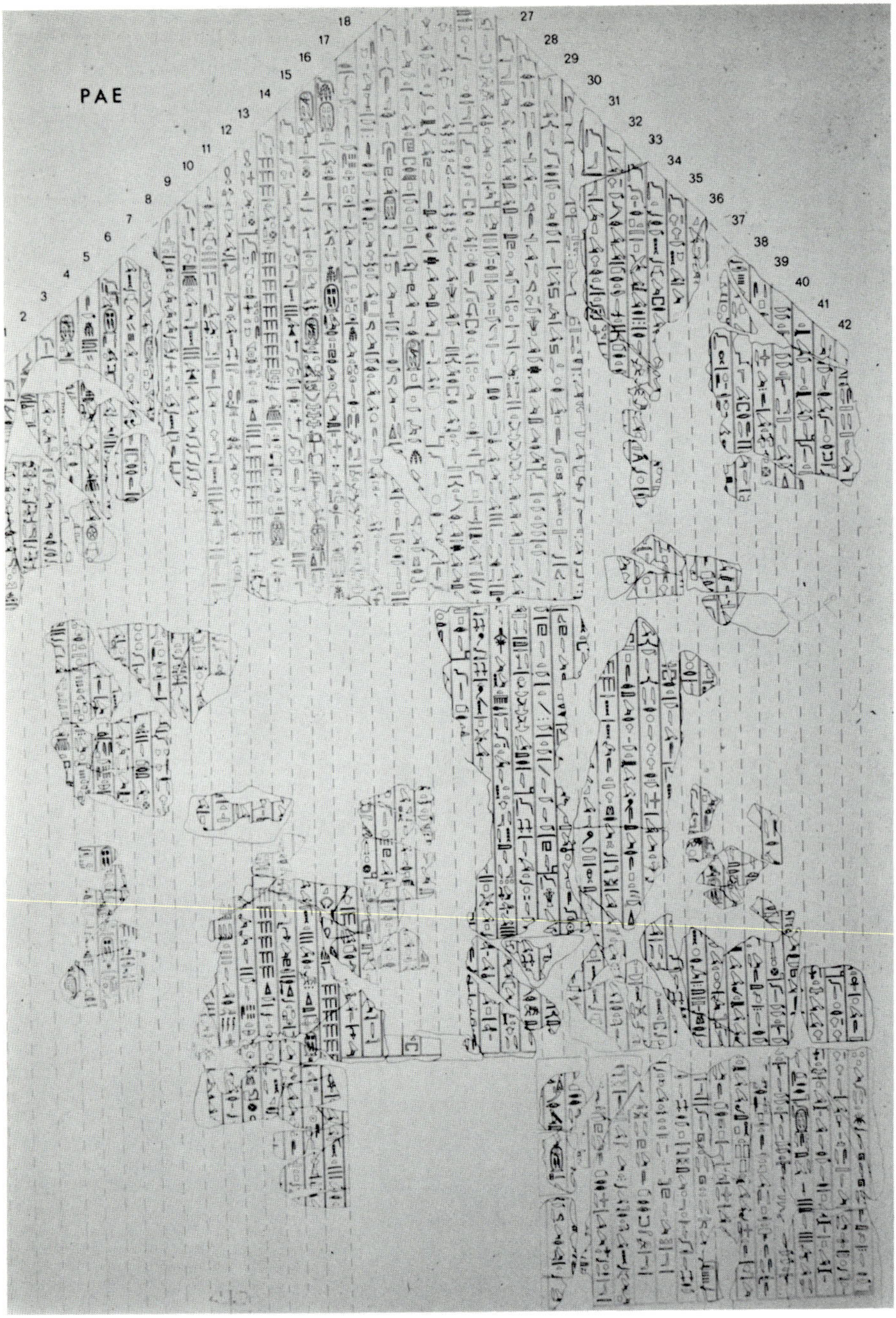

II b: Saqqarah. Pyramid of Pepi I. Drawings of texts reassembled from the East wall of the antechamber (P/A/E).

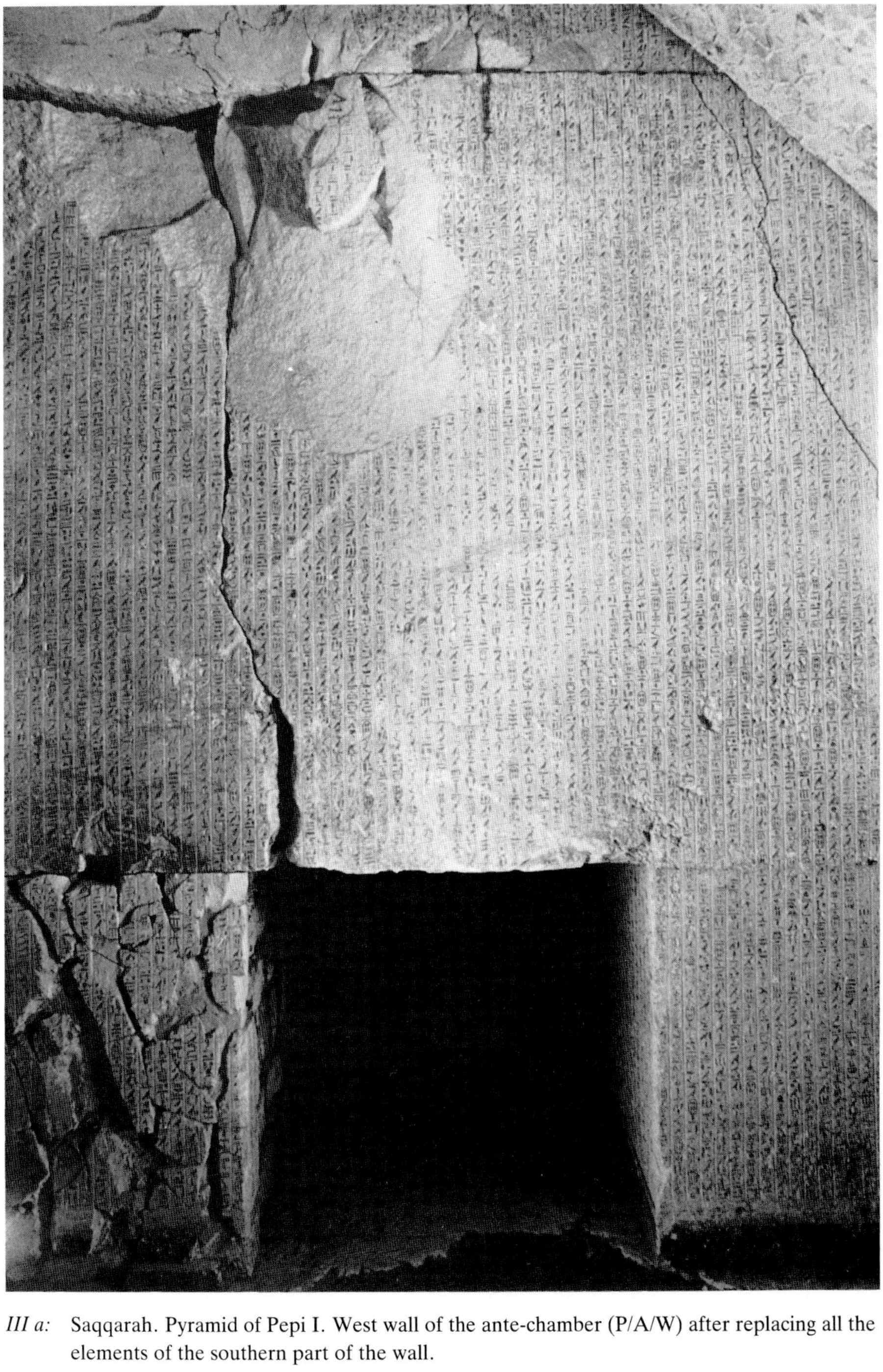

III a: Saqqarah. Pyramid of Pepi I. West wall of the ante-chamber (P/A/W) after replacing all the elements of the southern part of the wall.

III b: Saqqarah. Pyramid of Pepi I. Details of the text of the pyramids: the back part of the lion has been plastered, while only the front part has been painted; the hieroglyphic signs is present for reading purposes but magically the animal can do no harm.

IV a: Saqqarah. Funerary temple of Pepi I while being cleared. View from the West-East axis.

It is in the following way that a vast quantity of publications on the Pyramid Texts have been prepared by our expedition: the inscriptions themselves with all their numerous new supplements, comments and the translation. Little by little, to the extent that it was possible and in order to mark out the progressive steps of our work, we published some elements of reconstitutions in the following works: *Revue d'Egyptologie*, 27, 1975, p. 137–149; *Comptes rendus de l'Académie des Inscriptions et Belles-Lettres*, 1977, p. 269–288; *Scholae A. de Buck Memoriae dicatae*, Leiden, 1979; *Festschrift E. Edel*, Bamberg, 1979, p. 285–301; *Studies in Egyptian Religion J. Zandee*, 1982, p. 76–88.

The purpose of the Pyramids Texts is essentially to insure the resurrection of the Pharaoh – and this in the most pressing way, by all means. In fact, they associate a collection of ill-assorted formulae of various origins and of different functions. The shape of the Pharaoh being reborn can be conceived in different ways: inhumation in the sand, in a mastaba made of bricks, under a pyramid built of stones; osirian rebirth (the Pharaoh being the king of the dark spaces of an underground world), solar ascending (the king, companion of Re's boat, navigates in the sky), the star's eternity (the king, like a star, shines endlessly among the circumpolar stars). Other texts are of different nature: sometimes the dead participate in human form in the offerings and in the cult, sometimes the soul seems separated from the body and to have a different destiny. But there are also numerous references to purifications, fumigations, anointings, dressing, bringing of offerings, and this would indicate that some texts were conceived for recitations during the inhumation and the offering rituals. There are also texts of incantations against the evil powers, in the shape of wild bulls or dangerous snakes. Thus, those texts contain concepts that are much anterior to the time they were written and it gives us some light on more ancient periods of the pharaonic civilization.

Together, research on the graphic and grammatical peculiarities of the Pyramid Texts were undertaken. Hieroglyphs, which represent among other things human figures and animals, being an animated writing, one had to be careful that none of those signs could be interpreted against the Pharaoh and thus placing him in a bad situation in the other world. Therefore, the signs representing man or parts of the human body were avoided as much as possible or reduced to harmless elements: in *houi* 'to strike', the armed man is simply symbolized by a stick which is kept (sometimes not) with the arm. The interdictions were also extended to the animals, the bulls or the lions; the body of the lion is cut into two parts. On the East wall of the antechamber of Pepi I, images of lions, bovines, elephant or giraffe are subject to a peculiar practice: the outline of the sign is entirely engraved, then the rear has been carefully plastered, only the front part is painted, and thus the eventual dangerous animal is at the same time present in the graphic system and mutilated in a magic way.

After the philology, let us proceed to the archeological aspect of the site. The pyramid is in fact only one element of a vast group: the pyramidal complex. At the border of the lower land, at the limit of the cultivated fields, is located the temple of the valley or welcoming temple, where the funerary boats landed; a very long causeway goes upward, on the edge of a desert cliff, toward the funerary temple. Thus on the Eastern side of the pyramid of Pepi I, we have studied the funerary temple while having to clear considerable remains. That temple has the advantage that it had never been investigated before by our predecessors. On the other hand, this temple has a considerable importance: it is the most venerable sanctuary of the memphite region: "Pepi is stable of perfection", Pepi-men-nefer – Mennefer gave its name to Memphis itself.

The excavations revealed the fact that the temple was much destroyed. We have, however, discovered storage rooms of which the first floor remained, something very exceptional for a ruin of that period. As is commonly done for this type of building, it was built with a surrounding wall and was made of two parts: an open part (entrance hall, portic square, storage rooms) and another that can be qualified as being more private (chapel with five niches for statues, sanctuary for offerings). Communication was ensured by long narrow corridors. The rooms did not exceed a width of 5,20 m, due to the difficulties presented by supporting the roofing elements. From the entrance, at the top of the ascending causeway, one could reach, via a long hall, a courtyard with a peristyle with square pillars supporting the portico. A great number of fragments of the original decoration have been preserved, in particular reliefs of the offerings rooms. A collection of statues of "prisoners", kneeling, arms tied in the back, were gathered. They represent faces of the South and Northern countries and form a beautiful gallery for ethnographic studies. It is also a valuable collection of art of the Ancient Empire. Those statues had been cut into pieces in order to be put in lime kilns. There were also statuettes of the Middle Empire bearing the names and titles of the priests performing the funerary cult; they testify to the reoccupation of the temple at the beginning of the Middle Empire, more exactly at the time of Prince Sesostris-ankh. It is a precious testimony concerning a later revival of the cult of the Pharaohs of the Ancient Empire. In conclusion, the excavation of the temple of Pepi I provides historical elements of great interest in addition to the information so valuable for the knowledge of the archeology and the religion of Pharaonic Egypt.

Luigi Cagni (Istituto Universitario Orientale, Naples)

HISTORY, ADMINISTRATION AND CULTURE OF ACHAEMENID MESOPOTAMIA

Status of Current Studies

Considering the nature and scope of this extraordinary Congress in which more than 1800 researchers and scholars are participating, and for which more than 800 papers have been accepted, it seemed most opportune to make my report on Mesopotamia in the Achaemenid Period as brief as possible, as well as to develop it schematically along essential lines which would be easily comprehensible. In light of this my paper can be but a brief survey of the current situation in these studies.*

1. The Conquest of Babylon and Extension of the Persian Empire

It seems to me that the beginning of our discussion about Mesopotamia in the Achaemenid Period must take note of the year 539 B.C. In that year, shortly after becoming king of Persia, Cyrus II the Great, managed to conquer Babylon "without a battle".[1] In that moment, after three thousand years of independence, Mesopotamia definitively fell under foreign domination and permanently ceased being the political axis and centerpoint of oriental culture. Persia of the Achaemenids took up this historic role for two centuries (539–331 B.C.) before handing on the palm to the Greece of Alexander the Great and the Seleucids, and to other nations after them.

However, the ascendancy of the Persians around the middle of the sixth century B.C. also signified, in a brief span of years, a decisive expansion of its borders towards the East as well as the West, with the result that it created "the first world empire" (R. Ghirshman).[2] With the Babylonian conquest, the natural and historical barrier between Mesopotamia and Iran, the Zagros mountain

* I suppose, not having the chance of reading it, that the content of the book *Kunst, Kultur und Geschichte der Achämenidenzeit und ihr Fortleben,* H. Koch and D. N. Mackenzie (eds.), Berlin 1983, is close to my paper's title.

1 See the citation of the "Chronicle of Nabonidus" at the end of this paper.

2 R. Ghirshman, *L'Iran dès origines à l'Islam*, Paris 1951 and 1976, p. 13 (Abbrev.: *Iran*).

chain, was, so to speak, levelled. The Achaemenid rulers extended their conquests to central and western Asia (India), reaching China's borders with Darius I (522–486 B.C.).

As for the West, Cyrus (559–530 B.C.) had added the conquest of Anatolia and Syria to that of Babylon. His son, Cambyses (530–522 B.C.), conquered Egypt and Cyprus. After Darius I (522–486 B.C.) had carried out his great conquests of the East, he made Lybia the western border of the empire, and fought with the Greeks and the Scythians across the Black Sea.[3]

It is worth noting that, according to some modern scholars, the invention of the notion of 'emperor' occurred only with Darius I (522–486 B.C.).[4] From these facts, the definition given of ancient Iran seems more than justified: "Un pays charnière entre l'Occident et l'Orient".[5]

2. *Research Questions*

In the face of this radical political change of the East and part of the West, and particularly the fact that Mesopotamia, having lost its independence, became a "province" of a foreign empire for the first time, scholars of various disciplines, in particular Assyriologists (together with students of Iran and the Near East) are always interested in the problems and inquiries which we discuss here. Their intention is to appreciate better what were the actual conditions of Mesopotamia during Achaemenid domination in regard to politics, administration, religion and culture in general.

Specific questions concern the relation of Mesopotamia to Iran, as well as the survival and transformation of Mesopotamian civilization in the Achaemenid Period.

3 Cf. R. Ghirshman, *Iran*, p. 13. A. L. Oppenheim, *Ancient Mesopotamia* ..., Chicago 1964, p. 388.

4 This thesis was held with insistence by Cl. Herrenschmidt in various articles, for example "La première royauté de Darius avant l'invention de la notion d'empire", in Ph. Gignoux et alii, *Pad nām i yazdān*, Paris 1979, pp. 23–33; "L'Empire perse achéménide", in M. Duverger (ed.), *Le concept d'Empire*, Paris 1980, pp. 69–102.

5 The jacket cover of Ghirshman's book, 1976.

3. Lack of Documentation and Studies

We must immediately confess that our knowledge still has many lacunae, regarding both the amount of documents and the careful investigation of them. This applies first of all to the Persian empire, as M. W. Stolper rightly affirms:

> Despite the priority of the Achaemenid royal inscriptions in the history of cuneiform studies, much of the internal history of the Achaemenid Empire remains in shadow. While the period of the Persian Empire's growth is amply documented, sources from its mature years, after the dramatic reigns of Cyrus II and Darius I, are sparse and disparate.[6]

The situation is certainly no better for Mesopotamia in the Achaemenid Period. Compared to other periods, its study has been neglected for too long for a series of reasons, which we cannot discuss here. It is enough to recall, as an excellent example, that the 1,404 texts in the British Museum dated to the reigns of Cyrus, Cambyses and Darius published only in cuneiform copy by J. N. Strassmaier in 1890–1892 have never been systematically investigated nor carefully explained in their global content (that is, administrative, juridic, economic, commercial and religious dimensions). The same could be said for more than 2,000 other texts like those of Strassmaier, the overwhelming majority of which have economic-administrative content.

Since these are the primary documents from Mesopotamia, it is clear that the lack of adequate investigation of such material deprives us of much knowledge that we could otherwise gain. Undoubtedly precious though partial studies of texts under various aspects done many years ago are associated with such prestigious names as J. Augapfel, G. Cardascia, E. Ebeling, J. Kohler, A. B. Moldenke, E. W. Moore, F. E. Peiser, M. San Nicolò, K. L. Tallqvist, R. C. Thompson, A. Ungnad, S. Weingort etc. Cuneiform copies of texts were authored by these and many other scholars, among them J. Augapfel, A. T. Clay, G. Contenau, R. Ph. Dougherty, H. H. Figulla, C. E. Keiser, O. Krückmann, A. Pohl, A. Tremayne etc.

In his 1974 book dedicated to slavery in Babylon, M. A. Dandamayev calculated that the securely dated Achaemenid Mesopotamian texts published at least in cuneiform copy (and in some sense otherwise known) would amount to 3,545. To these could be added those which presumably belong to the same period though they are not dated.[7] Moreover, Dandamayev estimates that the sum of dated texts for the Neo-Babylonian and Achaemenid Periods taken together is

6 M. W. Stolper, *Management and Politics in Later Achaemenid Babylonia: New Texts from the Murašû Archive* (*Volumes I and II*), Doctoral dissertation in the University of Michigan, Ann Arbor 1974, p. ii. (Abbrev.: *Management*).

7 M. A. Dandamayev, *Slavery in Babylonia in the 7th–4th Centuries B.C. (623–331 B.C.)* (in Russian), Moscow 1974, pp. 7–12.

7,003. The number of undated texts, which also include a few post-Achaemenid examples, is 9,778. Finally, he has calculated that about 10,000 texts belonging to the same two periods lie unedited in various museums.

4. The Recent Reawakening of Studies

Though all of this is sadly true, we must recognize that the last ten years have witnessed a new appreciation of and interest in studies on Achaemenid Mesopotamia. I will limit myself to three significant statistics to exemplify this.

1) The first concerns the publication of many new texts. As the same M. A. Dandamayev reported two months ago at the International Assyriological Conference at Leiden, the Mesopotamian cuneiform texts of the Neo-Babylonian and Achaemenid Periods have risen from 9,778 (above) to 13,096, and increase of 3,318 texts. Letters written between 600–450 B.C. have risen from 749 in 1974 to 861, an increase of 112. For the reigns of Cyrus, Cambyses and Darius, 512 texts have been added.

2) The second statistic regards the numerous scholars who are expressing more interest in Achaemenid Mesopotamian literature. Some of the principal names are: P. Briant, M. D. Coogan, M. A. Dandamayev, R. B. Dillard, J.-M. Durand, H. Freydank, H. Hunger, J. Krecher, H. M. Kümmel, H. Lanz, J. Joannès, J. Oelsner, G. Ries, E. Salonen, M. W. Stolper, E. N. von Voigtlander, R. Zadok.

3) The third statistic concerns the Achaemenid Project which I direct. In 1974, thinking about the general situation of Assyriological studies, I came to the conclusion that it might be opportune to initiate an "Achaemenid Project". After a timid beginning in 1975 under the chair of Assyriology at the Istituto Universitario Orientale of Naples, with the support of the National Council for Research (Consiglio Nazionale delle Ricerche, Rome), the Project has grown stronger in successive years.

Above all, the Project proposes to publish all known texts from previous collections in transliteration and translation with a modest commentary. Eventually unedited texts would be added. Afterwards, and partly contemporaneously, the Project will produce monographs. Finally, it will propose an historical, economic, religious and cultural synthesis of Achaemenid Mesopotamia.

Since more than 4,000 texts are known today, we agree that the Project seems somewhat ambitious and will take many years. Three doctoral degrees have already been awarded in conjunction with the Project.[8] The first two col-

8 G. Giovinazzo on the texts of Cyrus by Strassmaier; L. Rossi and V. Ibello on the texts of Darius by Strassmaier.

laborators, Doctors Simonetta Graziani and Grazia Giovinazzo, the latter present at this Congress, have recently published their investigations of three groups of texts.[9] A volume which will publish Strassmaier's 384 texts of Cyrus is nearing the final stages of preparation.

5. *Some Themes of Recent Research*

Keeping in mind the methodology I mentioned in the beginning, I wish to conclude my report by briefly highlighting some themes pertaining to the history, administration, religion and culture of Achaemenid Mesopotamia. After examining the most recent literature, these themes appear to me to be particularly relevant and worthy of consideration.

1. *Chronological Distribution of Texts* – It remains true that the majority of Achaemenid documents coincide with the political reigns of the Achaemenid rulers: Cyrus – Cambyses – Darius I (539–486 B.C.). Among other texts, two new groups belonging to the period after Darius I are worthy of mention. The first group of 102 texts was published by M. W. Stolper in the second part of his *Management and Politics in Later Achaemenid Babylonia: New Texts from the Murašû Archive* (*Volumes I and II*). These texts of the Murašû family shed new light on the period of 455–403 B.C., the working years of this family of businessmen. We must also keep in mind that "in Babylonia, a major source of information on the later decades of the Empire is the Murašû Archive" (Stolper).[10]

The second group from Nippur-Šâṭir consists of 47 texts, some of which were already known. All but one are dated to the reign of Artaxerxes II (404–359 B.C.). They are very interesting since 24 are literary pieces (lists of plants, stones, divinities, letters, a ritual etc.). F. Joannès has studied this group with particular reference to the other 23 economic texts.[11]

2. *Geographical Origins of the Texts* – Babylon, Uruk, Nippur, Borsippa, Sippar, Ur etc. continue to furnish the greater number of texts. However, there have been important advances in giving more precision, such as the group of 35 "Texts of Nippur and Its Region" studied by F. Joannès.[12] Thanks to these texts,

9 G. Giovinazzo, "La 'cerimonia della vestizione' (*lubuštu*) nei testi achemenidi datati al regno di Ciro", *AION* 41 (1981), pp. 527–559; "28 testi economici della Mesopotamia datati al regno di Ciro" (= A. Pohl, *AnOr* 8–9), *AION* 43 (1983), pp. 533–589; S. Graziani, "I testi mesopotamici achemenidi del regno di Ciro contenuti in BE VIII", *AION* 43 (1943), pp. 1–31.

10 M. W. Stolper, *Management*, p. ii.

11 F. Joannès, *Textes économiques de la Babylonie récente* (Etudes Assyriologiques, Cah. n° 5), Paris 1982, pp. 1–110 (Abbrev.: *TEBR*).

12 F. Joannès, *TEBR*, pp. 1ff.

we know the region of Šâṭir much better. What is more important, these texts have better clarified the character of administration of the region, with particular reference to the feudal organization set up there by Cyrus II in regard to civil life, and by Cambyses in regard to military life. During the time of Artaxerxes II (404–359 B.C.), the feudal organization cast a shadow on the activity of the Temple of Ekur and the local civil administration.

3. *Typology of the Texts* – Economic-administrative texts predominate as always. As mentioned earlier, the private letters identified have increased from 749 in 1974 to 861.

4. *Archives* – The International Assyriological Conference at Leiden last July had as its theme: Cuneiform Archives and Libraries. M. A. Dandamayev stated: "With a few exceptions we do not possess state archives of the Neo-Babylonian and Achaemenid Periods". The archives of those periods are either from the temple, from families (Egibi, Murašû), or even private persons.

5. *Art, Court Ceremonial, and Royal Titles of the Achaemenid Kings* – Recent studies are confirming that various elements of art, court ceremonial and royal titles of the Achaemenid kings clearly manifest Mesopotamian influence. However, further study in this matter is desirable. The titles (particularly one recalls *šāh-ān-šāh*, "king of kings", Akkadian *šar šarrāni*) "are patterned on models from Urartu, which in their turn follow the formulary of the Assyrian Chancery" (Gh. Gnoli).[13] This judgment has been recently confirmed by B. Kienast.[14]

6. *Privileged Consideration of Babylon* – The city and region of Babylon, and indeed all of Mesopotamia, enjoyed privileged consideration in the vast empire on the part of the Achaemenid kings. Beyond what was said in the preceding point, it is worth recalling that Babylon was already chosen by Cyrus II as one of his capitals (together with Susa and Ecbatana in addition to the royal residence at Pasargade). The same ruler established his first-born son there with the title "king of Babylon".[15]

The abundant economic documentation clearly, though indirectly, shows the particular favorable behavior of the Achaemenid kings toward Babylon. From these records, the administrative establishment of the previous, Neo-Babylonian, period is fully confirmed.

7. *Civil and Religious Policies of Cyrus* – The last point in our survey deserves to be dedicated to the civil and, above all, the religious policies of Cyrus. These policies have been represented as markedly liberal, tolerant and farsighted by

13 Gh. Gnoli, in *Gururājamañjarikā. Studi in onore di Giuseppe Tucci*, Napoli 1974, vol. I, p. 24.

14 B. Kienast, "Zur Herkunft der achämenidischen Königstitulatur", in U. Haarmann – P. Bachmann (eds.), *Die islamische Welt zwischen Mittelalter und Neuzeit* (Festschrift Hans Robert Roemer), Beirut 1979, pp. 351–364.

15 Cf. R. Ghirshman, *Iran*, p. 129.

more or less concurrent ancient sources (Mesopotamian and biblical), as well as by modern scholars. There are two principal Mesopotamian sources which are highly laudatory.

The first is entitled the "Chronicle of Nabonidus". It states that the conquest of Babylon took place without conflict, and that the entrance of Cyrus into the city was seen as that of a benefactor.

On the sixteenth day (of the month Tišri) (= 12 October), Ugbaru, governor of the Guti, and the army of Cyrus entered Babylon without a battle (. . .). On the third day of the month Markešvan (= 29 October) Cyrus entered Babylon. They (= the Babylonians) filled the *ḫa-ri-né-e* [16] before him. The state of peace was imposed upon the city. Cyrus decreed the state of peace to all Babylon. Gubaru, his district officer, appointed district officers in Babylon.[17]

The second source is the "Cylinder of Cyrus". It contains a Babylonian inscription which, in the passage which interests us, speaks of the call of Cyrus by Marduk.

He (i.e. Marduk) scanned and looked (through) all the countries searching for a righteous ruler willing to lead him (in the annual procession). (Then) he pronounced the name of Cyrus, king of Anšan, declared him (lit. pronounced his name) to be(come) the ruler of all the world.[18]

The religious policy of Cyrus, and at least some of his successors,[19] is an important theme in the study of the relations between Mesopotamia and Iran. As mentioned already, until now this has been evaluated quite positively.

However, recent studies have encouraged a realistic second look at this position. In particular, I am alluding to some considerations which emerged in the Colloquium at Groningen in 1981, which had as its theme: "Cyrus the Great and the Beginning of the Persian Empire". See how much was devoted to the religious policy of Cyrus.

In the last two papers the traditional view of a mild and tolerant Cyrus was seriously questioned. Not only is tolerancy in itself an anachronistic concept, as has recently been argued by Tozzi (Rivista

16 *ḫa-ri-né-e ina pāni-šú umallû* (DIRI.MEŠ). As suggestive as the translation, "green twigs were spread in front of him", held by A. L. Oppenheim in *ANET*, p. 306 and note 13, and proposed again in *CAD*, Ḫ, p. 102 ("They filled the streets with branches in front of him"), is, it is not accepted today because the significance of the hapaxlegomenon *ḫarinû* remains obscure.

17 Col. III, 15–16, 18–20. See recently K. Grayson, *Assyrian and Babylonian Chrinicles*, Locust Valley, N.Y., 1975, pp. 109–110.

18 Cuneiform text in 5 R 35, 11–12. Cfr. A. L. Oppenheim, *ANET*, p. 315.

19 One thinks of Darius I (522–486 B.C.) who showed himself to be very liberal towards the temple of Apollo in Magnesia, as the letter written by him to the satrap Gadata shows. This document is preserved for us only in Greek, and is dated to the second century A.D. However, the document appears to be authentic and, consequently, goes back to the sixth century B.C. Cfr. J. Briend – J.-M. Seux, *Textes du Proche-Orient et Histoire d'Israël*, Paris 1977, pp. 155–156. With Xerxes I (486–465 B.C.), there is a change in Persia's behavior toward Babylon.

Storica Italiana 31 (1978), 26f.), a careful comparison with Assyrian data, presented by *van der Spek*, also shows that Cyrus' behaviour is in most cases precedented by that of Assyrian kings. Even the fact that Cyrus as well as his successors outside Iran never mention the name of their own god is not so unique as has been thought. Far too little importance has been attached to the continuance of Mesopotamian traditions by the Persian kings.[20]

The question merits further investigation.

6. Conclusion

These examples, among the many which could be noted, suffice to show how much fruit attentive research on various aspects of the civilization of Achaemenid Mesopotamia can and ought to bear. At the same time, they remind us how far we have yet to go.

20 H. W. A. M. Sancisi-Wendenburg, *Persica* 10 (1982), p. 274.

R. Morton Smith (University of Toronto)

NAMES AND KINGSHIP IN VEDIC INDIA

"Gentlemen's names and their implications" would be a better title. Vedic India lasts long, only petering out about the 3rd century B.C. I suggest that more information on Ancient India is available from names than has been extracted. Names are serious matters, and are likely to reflect beliefs and practices, and changes in them; and satire may appear in the nicknames which have stuck – a class very common in Italy, where the family system preserved them. Our evidence is very limited; till the rise of the heresies the vast majority of names we have are male, even more emphatically brahman or kṣatriya. There is no clear distinction between these varnas, which supports the view of their early identity of personnel. Names in RV are textually secure (whether they should be or not); in the Brahmanas there are some variants. Textual problems arise in the later brahmanical writings. In the secular world some names are available in cuneiform transcription in the Mesopotamian area, with some choice in interpretation. In the Purana the Ms variation is often troublesome; my *Dates & Dynasties* attempts to establish a critical text for the kings on critical and historical principles. Some names remain highly doubtful; there is a tendency in the later Puranas to make them more correct in terms of brahmanical theory: the KrṣṇaVāsudeva portion is especially dubious and troublesome. In the Brāhmana, the VB and JUB vamšas give personal names, but elsewhere we are very liable to be left with family names; these go back to personal names, but how long previously? (e.g. Saukarāyaṇa, Bhāradvājīputra). Personal names may also be lost under sobriquets and nicknames (though these do carry information). Names can also be assumed, e.g. Janamejaya III seems to have assumed Sattrajit, and synonyms seem sometimes substituted. Having said all this, we still think the study of names can tell us something.

In early society names were a reality, hence giving them a serious business; given in a religious ceremony they may carry the magical force of the sacred language, and be self-fulfilling. For meanings RV meanings are going to be preferable to classical, but attestations are limited. Categories of names often overlap, and placing is ambiguous, e.g. Ketu may have astronomical or kṣatriya connotation, (born under a comet/meteor; or Chief; or be a hypocoristic). Archaism of word or form may survive in names, e.g. king Viṁša may show rt. Lat. Vinco, conquer; the compound type Jamad-agni, Bharadvāja disappears early.

The same types of names may be found among most Indo-European peoples, but it would seem very few identical even between Iranian and Indian. Gk. and Skt. share Eteocles, Echecles, Eumenes (*Fehu-*) Satyašravas, Sahašravas, Vasumanas; but though very few are identical, it is not unreasonable to look for etymology beyond the individual language, e.g. king Alarka does suggest connection with alalkē/alalkomenos of Gk. So too while añjana = lizard or lamp-black, Gk. engonos Born in the family, explains better.

Truth is an important religious entity for kings in I-E times. The name Eteocles is the remaining trace in Greece, where the Classical conception has changed. Satya is a common first element in Skt., and we have Satyajit as late as 630. With the secularized kingship of the Formative period the old truth loses its importance, but we find a handful of names in Satya- with the brahmanical revival, e.g. Satyadāman Ksatrapa c. A.D. 190. In Iran it might seem that Arta – – replaced Satya – – under Zoroastrian influence. Rta is very common in Iran, but it seems to be connected with Varuna and decline with him in India. We have Rtadhvaja alternative for Kuvalašva c. 1290, Rta with v.l. Kratu Janaka c. 520, and a v.l. Rtaṁjaya for Raṇaṁjaya or better Rṇaṁj/caya Aikṣvāka c. 560. Rtadhāman is known under Manu Sāvarni whatever that means, but the name occurs among the Mitanni, ar ta ta a ma; we also have there Rtasmara, Rtamna, Rtamănya (Ar ta su ma ra, ar ta am na, ar ta ma an ia) Rtabhāga is guaranteed by the patronymic in BAU before 600, but how long before? Dharma, which might be expected to take its place, and does appear in religious names from the 5/4th century, and in some royal names of the 5/6th A.D. – and these names may be assummed on entering the religious life, or on coronation, e.g. (Šīlāditya Dharmāditya) – does not necessarily or preferably have the religious sense in our period, but connection with Lat. FIRMUS, is much better.

We may next consider theophorics, which we may divide into those in which man is inferior to the gods, and those in which he is equal/superior; these we may divide as direct names or epithets/titles of the god, or compounds with his name. Theophorics with the god's name are remarkably few – we found only 40 – out of 2000. Strangely, this applies also to Homer in Greece, 5 plus 2 doubtful.

Names where the god is superior are early and especially late, depending on the rise of theism; they naturally drop while the gods are losing importance. This kind of theophoric is the only one in the Semitic world of the time, but rare in India. We have Indrota c. 1150 and (a brahman) 895 and in Mitanni; Indrapramati (also brahman). Ya mi u/o ta, Helped by the Twins occurs in Mitanni. Brahmadatta of 1090 is factual, not theophoric, the right mantra had produced him. Somadatta are 1120 & 1020, 1090. We have Su war da ta, equivalent to Súryadatta whom we find in ŠankhAr. probably after 600 B.C. There is Viṣṇuvrddha c. 1390, and Devarāta of 1420 & 1240, and Marutta, 1400, 1290, 1280. From c. 600 on such theophorics become commoner, Agnidatta, Aryamarādha, Bhavatrāta, Brhaspatigupta, Candragupta, Rudragupta, Kṛṣṇadatta, Kṛṣṇarāta, Mahīdāsa, Šarvadatta; -mitra may now show dependence, e.g. Agni-Surya-, Puṣan-, Indra-, Viṣṇu-, Prajāpati-, Varuṇa-, Phalguni-, Dhruva-, Puṣya-, Jyeṣṭha-, Brhatsvati-, the last five being astrological and after 300 B.C. In the Hindu resurgence of A.D. 200+ we have Indradatta, Indravarman, Rudravarman, etc.

Names of equality tend to disappear; e.g. we have Mitravarcas c. 240. Kṛṣṇadhrti 390, Raudrabhuti (possibly Rudr) 150, but if we go earlier such we find Indra common, often in names of brahmans. Before 800 we have Indrābha, Indradyumna, Indrabhū, Indradhanvan, Indrasena. In Mitanni we have Indrātithi, In ta ra at ti, also Suri a at ti & Mi tar(a) at ti, (Surya-/Mitra-atithi). In India we have Mitrātithi 1180. We have also Mitrabhū 1050, Devamitra 800, Devātithi 1040, Devāpi 1050 & 920, Somāpi c. 800. It is worth noting how few gods appear, and which are absent, e.g. Rudra, Šiva, Viṣṇu (once only). In some cases the theophoric is not clear, e.g. Mitrasaha, winning in the compact.

There would seem to be some direct god-names, e.g. Agni (Aurva), Mitrāvaruṇa (Vasistha), Mātarišvan Kāṇva; we have Kubera Varakya c. 570. Gods under their epithets are less certain; e.g. a king should be watching man, but is Nrcaksa 810 & 705 Mitra? Divākara 850 is the sun (moving by the sky, rt. car?). But is the brahman Prabhākara Atreya the sun? or merely successful in getting fire? Is Anala 1120 Agni, or have we a hypocoristic? Brhaspati, Samvarta's brother of 1290 is factual, as a brahman he possesses the brh/brahma. Is Trinetra 720 Šiva? he could be astronomical, born under Šiva's asterism. We have Indrabhūti (Gautama) c. 530, having the power/wellbeing of Indra.

Hospitality was an important royal duty in the early society; with the professionalization and urbanization this ceases to be, and -atithi disappears from names; the last seems to be Prātithi c. 950; getting, securing by the contract of friendship becomes more important, and mitra becomes a common 2nd member, though some mitra names are old (Viṣ̌vamitra 1320, Šankhamitra (Raibhya) not before 1180, Sumitra 1160 & 1140, and a doubtful Purumitra.

The majority of names are of good omen, whether for peace, war or sacrifice but some seem purely descriptive, and there are animal and plant names. Doubtless changes of fashion could be found. Thus horses seem to disappear after 800 whether as 1st or 2nd element; we have Ašvamitra Gobhila 480, and king Kinnarāšva c. 715, but I have found no more. The horse remains in Greek names perhaps due to the survival of chariot-racing. Strangely chariots are absent from Greek names (unless Eratosthenes contains one), but do well in Vedic times, disappearing with the old kṣatriya families; Dašaratha & Brhadratha Maurya can be classed with them or as archaisms. The chariot lasted long in the army, but there the elephant has taken prestige. Kings are expected to be warlike, and – sena is of continuous distribution.

The idea of one's rightful portion is Indo-European, hypostatized in the Aditya Bhaga. He fades, but there are traces of the conception, e.g. Ajamīḍha, Dvimīḍha, having the leader's/double portion. Bhagavitta shows a patronymic c. 780. Bhagiratha (possibly better Bhage-) would be having the chariot in his portion (as a king should).

Warlike names hardly need comment, and they are easily found on brahmans, e.g. Bharadvāja, Apnavâna, winning property, Iṣumant (patronymic 160) Rahuugaṉa, having a quick force of retainers, 1270, Sujayanta 370, not to mention Arinābha 1780, Jitāri 1320, Nrpañjaya 600, Janamejaya 1460, 1100, 950, 830, all kings/kṣatriyas. With these might go horse-names, e.g. Bahulašva, Šīghrašva, Trasadašva, Vadhryašva (important as not responding to mares in battle). So too with chariots. We have the brahman family Rathītara, better/overcoming the charioteer, Brhadratha, Apratiratha, Jayadratha (910). In Mitanni we have Abhiratha *a-bi-ra-at-ta*, the patronymic of Dašaratha, *da-a-sar(a)-ti*, Vrddhāšva *bar-da-aš-šu-a*, Priyāšva *bi-ri-aš-šu-wa* (Vīryāšva?) = Philippos.

Auspicious names are always in favour; Ayutāyus 1300, Arugvant 1160, Nirvrti 1210 & 730, Suvarcas 620, Suyašas 250, Brhadvasu 580, Adhrigu (not poor) RV. Ūrjayan strong, Vapuṣmant beautiful, (380&1060). In Mitanni we have Arhamana *a-ri-ha-ma-an-na* and Vandya *wa-an-di-ia*, to be honoured: Priya *bi-ri-a-a*, Narya *na-ri-ia*, Citra *zi-it-ra*, Puṇya *pu-ni-ia*, Citryarai, *zi-it-ri-ia-ri*, Subandhu, *su-ba-an-du*.

Important also to the kṣatriya is the ritual. We have Yajñasena, 1000, Yajñatura (Svikna) 1160; Šatayajña 820, Pracīnabarhis 1120, Somādhi 970. There are very many others, but such names might be expected to get fewer as the brahmans take over the ritual and as the ritual loses prestige with the heresies. My later names are mostly patronymics, and where not belong to brahmans, e.g. Suyajña Šāṇḍilya. However Višākhayūpa of Avanti c. 470 was royal. In Mitanni we have Candramyasta (later – miyedha) za an tar(a)mi as ta having a brillant sacrifice/offering. Guptāgni ku up ta ak ni might come here m having a protected (sacrificial) fire. In RV we have Dašòṇi c. 1180 haing 10 soma cups, ūṇi. Dadhivahana brings the curds for the sacrifice. Ulukhala, the mortar, ulmuka coal for kindling (the sacred fire) are found as names; We have king Sutapas 1280, and several Suhotras. Abhis(u)vant, pressing (the soma), Amšumant (having the soma stalks), Amšu, Āhuka, invoking, all partake in the ritual; is Ānarta doing the manly war dance? or Asamanjas properly Āsam-, anointing the altar (lat. āsa/ āra)? Ašmaka reminds one of the formula of the birth rite, 'Be an axe, be a stona ...'. We have Bali, Brhaddīksa, Brhaduktha, Brhanmedhas, Kambalabarhis, Satyakarman (having correct rites), and many more.

Auspicious names call for little comment; they continue right through, e.g. Siddhārtha (Gautama) 560, Sumitra 1190, 630, 400, Nanda/ivardhana 1460, 520, 460, 400. They apply in all spheres of life. Adhiratha will be a good chariot man, Atyamhas is beyond hurt; Ibhavant will have a prosperous house-hold and Purumitra many friends. Abhayada gives freedom from fear, as a king should; Susandhi and Dhruvasandhi will be admirable people, keeping their agreements.

But besides names auspicious and of good omen, there are a great many of mere fact, a kind common with Italic peoples, e.g. Lat. Quintus, Agrippa born feet first. So in Mitanni we have Kukṣya from the belly *ku-uš-ši-ya*, Šubhra *su-up-ra*, Itara *i-ta-ra*, Madhya *ma-ti-ia*. In India we have Nara (cf. Karl), Jana, Jāta, Nava, the new one, Kešin, hairy, big-eyes, Prthulākṣa, Dvita, Asitabāhu, white-armed, Gaya, the living creature, Rjūnas straight-nose, Okasa, Aurasa (i.e. of the house/body, not adopted or otherwise acquired). With these descriptive might go the astronomical, which we do not have yet in Mitanni, where we do get the factual like Bhrtya (cf. Bharata to be supported), *bi-ri-di-ia*, and apparently the Northerner & Easterner, *u-ti-az-zi-na*, *bi-ra-az-zi-na*, Udīcīna, Prācīna. We have Švetaketu born under a comet (?) like Rāhula at an eclipse, 542; Nidāgha of 1080 should be born in summer, Šišira (patr. 830) in winter, Aṣādha in that month. We have nakṣatras for Punarvasu, Proṣṭhapāda, Šakata (patr.); Ārdra of 1720 might be from the nakṣatra also, as it is attested in AV, and the system seems to go back to the Harappa culture. Daršaka might be born on the day of 1st sighting of new moon; the influence of astrology is perhaps to be seen in Puṣyamitra & Jyeṣṭhamitra Šunga.

Animal names are found throughout the Indo-European area, but in Skt. the animals are often surprisingly unprestigious – as evidently happens in Mesopotamia. There is Ahīnas (cf. Gk. echinos) the hedgehog. There are the tortoise, the mosquito, partridge, jackal, bear, goat, wolf, owl, strangely not the tiger or lion (kurma/kašyapa, mašaka, tittiri, kroṣṭuka, rkṣa aja/basta, ulūka, ula (=?). In Mitanni we have the owl *u-lu-uq-qa*, wolf *wi-ir-ri-ka*, tortoise *ku-ur-mi-ya*, and bull, rsabha *i-ri-is-a-bi*/*i-ri-i-sa-bi*, *i-ri-sa-ba*. There are many others, bird or beast, e.g. puṣkarasāda, Arṇa, birds. Cf. OIs orn, Gk. *orni-os*).

There seem to be too many plants to deny. Latin shows Piso, pea, Cicero, chick-pea, Tubero, tuber. Plant names are often not attested till late, but must have existed. There is a parallel in sense between Lat. Fabius and Mudgala/Maudgalya – the bean is an old and taboo vegetable for some. Not surprisingly I cannot find any in Mitanni, but in India we have before 800 Āmalaka, Āšvattha Badara (by patr.) Iṭa, Ikṣvāku, Mandāra, Mucukunda, Mūlaka. We have Nyagrodha, 980 and 280; there is gulgulu (by patr.), king Dūrva 580, and many others.

Finally many names seem to have begun as nicknames and become family names as in Latin, or at least superseded the original. Was Alīkayu 840 a little liar? or did he tell one big lie? Buḍila's ancestor (ante 820) was evidently ridiculous as he could only afford a mule for a horse, Aśvatarāśva. We have Hiranyadant Vaida 890. Gandūṣa of 1080 must have been always drinking from his hands. One would think Dīrghatamas of 1290 was not the child's born name, Kusīdin Kāṇva of RV seems already in the loan business. Such nicknames do not seem to be among the earliest names, but they continue late, e.g. Pulindaka Śunga, Śaliśūka Maurya, Lambodara Andhra; Lomapāda Yadava of 1260 could be fact, or could be a nickname, as Lomapāda Daśaratha is (Anga). Aktākṣa may have had some eye disease, and Kāṇḍviya the itch. Someone may have odd diet, berries or bamboo shoots, Pippilād(a), Karīrād(a).

The reason for some names will escape us, e.g. Pāśadyumna (RV): is it patr. onymic, rt/paś, shining eye? Jīmūta why? Some are not etymologizable to us, e.g. Sainmiṣi (JB), Śini. Some may be old, e.g. we may have Jājali in Mitannian *za-az-za-ri*. *Tu-ug-ra* should be RV Tugra. Asura seems to be a common element in Mitanni; the degrading of the Asuras is late and post Vedic. In India we have patronymics from Asura; but Asurātithi *aš-šu-ra at-ti*, Karmāsura *kal-ma-aš-šu-ra*, Bhedāsura (Vedic name Bheda) *be-ta-aš-šu-ra*, Avāsura, *a-u-a-aš-šu-ra*, for these we go to Mitanni.

We hope the foregoing may suggest to some the value of research on Personal names, as reflecting values and attitudes of society which would otherwise escape us. We may not get the same certainty as in grammatical studies, but we should not smother imagination by only accepting or considering documented records.

Appendix
Names and Kingship in Vedic India

ABHAYADA: giving freedom from fear
a-bi-ra-at-ta =
? ABHIRATHA: beside the chariot
? ABHIRĀTA: given (for a purpose)
ABHIṢ(U)VANT: pressing (soma)
ADHIRATHA: on the chariot, charioteer
ADHRIGU: not poor
AGNI: fire. The god Fire
AGNIDATTA: given by Agni
AGNIMITRA: having Agni as a friend
AHĪNAS: hedgehog
ĀHUKA: invoking (hypocoristic?)
AJA: leader or goat
AJABASTA: goat
AJAMĪḌHA: having the leader's reward
AKTĀKṢA: having smeared eyes/dice/axle
ALARKA: defending
ALĪKAYU: liar
ĀMALAKA: plant/fruit (myrobalan)
AMŚU: soma stalk. filament
AMŚUMANT: having the above
ANALA: fire
ĀNARTA: doing the manly dance
AÑJANA: born in the family
APNAVĀNA: winning wealth
APRATIRATHA: having no equal with the chariot
ĀRDRA: born under the 6th nakṣatra/? wet
ARHAMĀNA: worthy
ARINĀBHA: tearing the enemy
ARṆA: bird

ARUGVANṬ: without disease
ARYAMARĀDHA: gift of Aryaman
AṢĀḌHA: invincible/ born in month A.
ASAMAÑJAS: ? improper
ASITABĀHU: white-armed
AŚMAKA: stone
Asura, patr. ĀSURI; asura, lord
ASURĀTITHI: having an asura as guest
AŚVAMITRA: having his horse as friend
AŚVATARĀŚVA: having a mule for a horse
AŚVATTHA: tree, ficus religiosa
ATYAṀHAS: beyond harm
AURASA: (son) of the body
a-u-a-aš-šu-ra: lord of help/favour
AYUTĀYUS: having life of 10,000 (years)

BADARA: jujube, zizyphus jujuba
BAHULĀŚVA: having many horses
BALI: offering
BHAGAVITTA: having a found portion
BHAGĪ/ERATHA: having a splendid chariot/ having a chariot in his portion
BHARADVĀJA: carrying off the prize
BHAVATRĀTA: protected by Bhava/Śiva
BHARATA: to be supported, i.e. nurtured
BHEDA: destroyer
be-ta-aš-šu-ra: lord of destroying? better = ?VEDASURA, lord of sacred knowledge
BHRTYA: to be supported
BRAHMADATTA: given by the brahma power
BRHADDĪKṢA: having a great consecration
BRHADUKTHA: having a great hymn
BRHADRATHA: having a great chariot
BRHADVASU: having great wealth
BRHANMEDHAS: having a great sacrifice
BRHASPATI: lord of brahma power
BRHASPATIGUPTA: guarded by Brhaspati
BRHATSVĀTIMITRA: having the asterism B. as friend
BUḌILA: ?

CANDRAGUPTA: protected by the Moon
CANDRAMYAṢṬA: having a bright sacrifice
CITRA: bright
zi-it-ri-ia-ri = ? CITRYARAI: having brilliant wealth

DADHIVAHANA: bringing the curds (for the sacrifice)

DARŚAKA: born at 1st sight of new moon
DAŚARATHA: having 10 chariots
DAŚONI: having 10 soma cups
DEVAMITRA, DEVĀPI: having (the) gods as friends
DEVARĀTA: given by the/a god
DAVĀTITHI: having a god as guest
DHARMĀDITYA: sun of righteousness
DHRUVAMITRA: having the pole star as friend
DHRUVASANDHI: having a firm agreement
DĪRGHATAMAS: having long darkness
DŪRVA: a grass, panicum dactylon
DVIMĪḌHA: having double wage
DVITA: second

GAṆḌŪṢA: handful of water
GAYA: living creature
GOBHILA: fond of cows
GOTAMA: having most cows (wealth)
GUPTĀGNI: having a protected fire
GULGUDU: plant, bdellium

HIRAṆYADANT: having a golden tooth

IBHAVANT: having a (big) household
IKṢVĀKU; kind og gourd
INDRĀBHA: having the appearance of Indra
INDRABHŪ: having the being of Indra
INDRABHŪTI: having the prosperity of Indra
INDRADATTA: given gy Indra
INDRADYUMNA: shining like Indra
INDRADHANVAN: bow of Indra/having that
INDRAMITRA: having Indra as friend
INDRAPRAMATI: having care from Indra
INDRASENA: having Indra as his weapon
INDRĀTITHI: having Indra as guest
INDRAVARMAN: having Indra as his armour
IṢUMANT: having arrows
ITARA: other
IṬA: kind of reed/grass

JĀJALI: ?
JAMADAGNI: going to the (sacrifical) fire
JANA: human being
JANAMEJAYA: rousing the people
JĀTA: born
JAYADRATHA: overcoming the chariot
JĪMŪTA: cloud/plant, Luffa foetida?
JITĀRI: having conquered enemies

JYEṢṬHAMITRA: having the 16th (Indra's) nakṣatra as friend

KAMBALABARHIS: having a blanket for his sacrificial grass
KAṆḌVIYA: itchy
KARMĀSURA: lord of the sacrificial rite
KAŚYAPA: tortoise
KEŚIN: hairy
KINNARĀŚVA: having a kinnara for his horse
KROṢṬUKA: jackal
KṚṢṆADATTA: given by Kṛṣṇa
KṚṢṆADHṚTI: having his joy in Kṛṣṇa
KṚṢṆARĀTA: given by Kṛṣṇa
KUBERA: the godling K.
KUKṢYA: from the belly
KŪRMA: turtle

LAMBODARA: hanging belly
LOMAPÁDA: hairy leg

MADHYA: middle (hypocoristic?)
MAHĪDĀSA: having the earth as his servant
MANDĀRA: coral tree, Erythrina Indica
MARUTTA: given by the Maruts
MAŚAKA: gnat
MĀTARIŚVAN: the god M.
MITRABHŪ: having the being of Mitra
MITRASAHA: overcoming in the contract
MITRĀTITHI: having Mitra as a guest
MITRĀVARUṆA: the paired gods M. & V.
MUCUKUNDA: plant, pterospermum Suberifolium
MUDGALA: bean
MŪLAKA: root/radish

NANDA: joy
NANDIVARDHANA: increasing joy
NARA: male man
NARYA: manly
NAVA: the new one
NIDĀGHA: born in summer
NIRVṚTI: serene/satisfied
NṚCAKṢAS: seeing men
NṚPAÑJAYA: conquering kings
NYAGRODHA: banyan tree

OKASA: of the house

PHALGUNIMITRA: having the nakṣatra Ph. as friend
PRABHĀKARA: making light
PRĀCĪNA: easterner
PRĀCĪNABARHIS: having his sacrificial mat in the east
PRAJĀPATIMITRA: having Planet Jupiter as friend
PRĀTITHI: having guests in front/hospitable
PRIYA: dear (hypocoristic?)
PRIYĀŚVA: horse-loving
PROṢṬHAPĀDA: born under the nakṣatra P.
PṚTHULĀKṢA: wide-eyes
PULINDAKA: uncivilized tribe
PUNARVASU: born under P. nakṣatra
PUṆYA: auspicious
PŪṢĀMITRA: having Pūṣan as friend
PUṢKARASĀDA: kind of bird/bee?
PUṢYAMITRA: having P. nakṣatra as friend

RĀHŪGAṆA: having a swift entourage
RĀHULA: born at eclipse time
RATHĪTARA: overcoming the/better charioteer
ṚJŪNAS: straight-nose
ṚKṢA: bear
ṚṢABHA: bull
ṚTABHĀGA: having rta as his portion
ṚTADHVAJA: having rta as his banner
ṚTAMNA: mindful of rta
ṚTAMĀNYA/ĀRTAMANYA: honoured through rta, or patronymic of preceding? (*ar-ta-ma-an-ia*)
ṚTASMARA: remebering rta
RUDRABHŪTA: being as/by Rudra
RUDRAGUPTA: protected by Rudra
RUDRAVARMAN: having Rudra as his armour

SAHAŚRAVAS: having powerful fame
SAINMIṢI: ?
SAṀVARTA: meeting (an enemy)
SATTRAJIT: conquering in the sacrifice
SAUKARĀYAṆA: patr. of SŬKARA, doing well/boar
SATYADĀMAN: having a true gift/ having truth as his garland
SATYAKARMAN: having truth as his rite
SATYAŚRAVAS: having truth as his glory
SIDDHĀRTHA: having an attained purpose
SOMADATTA: given by Soma
SOMĀDHI: depositing the soma
SOMĀPI: havings Soma as friend

SUBHANDU: having good kindred
SUHOTRA: having a good oblation
SUJAYANTA: conquering easily
SUMITRA: having good friends/contract
SUSANDHI: having a good agreement
SŪRYADATTA: given by Sūrya (sun-god)
SŪRYAMITRA: having Sūrya as his friend
SŪRYĀTITHI: having Sūrya as guest
SUTAPAS: having good tapas (austerities)
SUYAJÑA: having a good sacrifice
SUVARCAS: having good energy

ŠAKAṬA: cart (man)
ŠĀLIŠŪKA: awn of rice
ŠĀṆḌILYA: ?
ŠAÑKHAMITRA: having the 'battle conch as friend'
ŠATAYAJÑA: doing 100 sacrifices
ŠARVADATTA: given by Šarva
ŠĪGHRĀŠVA: having a swift horse
ŠILĀDITYA: sun of good behaviour
ŠINI: ? (moving, cf. Gk. *kineō*?)
ŠIŠIRA: born in winter
ŠUBHRA: splendid
ŠUṄGA: a tree
ŠVETAKETU: having a white banner

TITTIRI: partridge
TRINETRA: 3-eyed
TRASADAŠVA: before whom horses flee

TUGRA: striking

?UDĪCĪNA: northerner
ULMUKA: firebrand
ULŪKA: owl
ULUKHALA: mortar or cup for soma
ŪRJAYAN: getting strong

VADHRYAŠVA: having gelded horses
VANDYA: to be honoured
VAPUṢMANT: handsome
VARUṆAGUPTA: protected by Varuṇa
VARUṆAMITRA: having Varuṇa as friend
VASUMANAS: well-disposed
VEDA: knowing
VIṀŠA: conquering
VIŠĀKHAYŪPA: having an unbranching sacrifical post
VIṢṆUGUPTA: protected by Viṣṇu
VIṢṆUMITRA: having Viṣṇu as friend
VIŠVĀMITRA: having everyone as friend
VIṢṆUVRDDHA: increased by Viṣṇu
VRDDHĀŠVA: having grown horses
VRKA: wolf

YADU: ?
YAJÑASENA: having the sacrifice as weapon
YAJÑATURA: overcoming in the sacrifice
ya-mi-u/o-ta: helped by the twins/charioteers

There are alternatives to some of these translations, both by various meanings of words, and the ambiguities of Sanskrit compounds. Some names are more ritual, some less so than they seem; e.g. *satya* has its importance as a ritual rather than a moral requirement for kings.

Ph. Gignoux (École Pratique des Hautes Études, Sorbonne, Paris)

CHURCH-STATE RELATIONS IN THE SASANIAN PERIOD

The constitution of a state religion in the Sasanian Iran from the 3rd century onwards and the excellent relations which it maintained with the monarchy during the whole period of the 3rd to the 7th century A.D. are now largely accepted views and held to be historically true, in spite of some shades of opinion, by all scholars in this field. This unanimous agreement on the very close link between the state and the church is of course borne out by numerous texts which bear witness to such a situation, but in my view a critical approach of these texts has been inadequately made. There are in fact two branches of sources which enlighten us in this field and which most probably owe something to each other. On the one hand the Pahlavi-Mazdean source, notably the Dēnkard which is definitely a later composition, and on the other hand the Arabo-Persian historiography with the Letter of Tansar, the writings of Masᶜūdī and the Testament of Ardachir all of which are obviously based on the Sasanian tradition, but which were not composed before the 10th century. But no one has really questioned how such late-dated texts could transmit to us trustworthy traditions of the 3rd century!

Let us consider first, in the main, the documents which have reached us in order to reconstruct the most likely historical reality before attempting to sketch a different picture of the relations between the church and the state.

I. Sources

A number of passages in the Dēnkard alluding to the association of kingship (*xvadāyīh*) and religion (*dēn*) are much more of a philosophical speculation than of a historical testimony, as is well-known. They describe, as Marijan Molé has pertinently remarked, a situation as it *should be* or as it will be when the world is restored at the end of the times. Chapter 58 in the Dēnkard III goes as far as identifying religion and kingship:

"Kingship is essentially religion[1] and religion kingship according to the teaching of the Good Religion. Even the enemies of this doctrine agree on this [basic] sentence, for they too profess that their kingship is based on religion and religion on kingship".[2]

The allusion here to the adherents of another religion, who closely associate secular power with religious authority, is clear enough. This doctrine is much more in accordance with Islam than with the Sasanians, which should therefore put us on guard. For we must ask ourselves if the Mazdean theologians did not simply think of a situation of their own times, that is to say, that of the Islamised Iran with unavowed regret that the union of religion and kingship was unhappily not made effective in the Sasanian period. We should, in any case, study this question in depth.

In another chapter in the Dēnkard III, translated by J. de Menasce, the same thing is repeated: "The Mazdean religion is the foundation of the power of kingship and as long as this religion is the ferment of kingship, the functioning of the authority of kingship will last".[3]

This idealisation of the union between kingship and religion most often refers not to a historical reality[4], but either to the regretted happy bygone mythical times or to the world to come which will see the dawn of peace and of eternal happiness thanks to the unfailing alliance of these two powers. On the one hand it is the image of the good kingship embodied by Yima and of the priesthood by Zoroaster.[5] On the other hand, according to the very apt comment on other chapters of the Dēnkard by M. Molé, "kingship and religion in their peak of intensity will only be reunited in the period of Sōšāns and only then the renewal will be able to set in."[6] M. Molé also affirms that "religion and kingship find themselves united in the same person,"[7] as demonstrated in DKM 129–130, but only for the eschatological future. He underlines at the same time the fact that, in the Pahlavi

1 Wherever it occurs, I have translated the word '*dēn*' by 'religion' for this is its basic meaning in these texts, keeping in mind the possibility of an eschatological connotation.

2 I have revised the translation given by M. Molé, *Culte, Mythe et Cosmologie dans l'Iran ancien*, Paris 1963, p. 51, where he wrongly translated *hambasān* by 'adhérent', and that of J. de Menasce, *Le troisième livre du Dēnkart*, Paris 1973, p. 65, which, on the whole, is accurate.

3 J. de Menasce, *ibid*. p. 319, Chapter 349.

4 The collaboration between the kings and religious leaders, stated by the Dēnkart, ed. Madan p. 140, is not a good enough argument, especially in the case of Ardashir and Tansar (whose historicity hasn't been proved, or, ar least, who probably didn't live in the third century), or of the alliance between Yazadgird I and Ādurbād ī Zarduštān, which is not mentioned anywhere else anyway: cf. M. *Molé*, ibid. p. 52.

5 See ch. 229 of the DK III, Molé p. 57 and J. de Menasce p. 241–243, which does indeed deal with the mythical origins of the alliance between religion and royalty with the example of Hōšang and Yima.

6 *Ibid*., p. 41.

7 *Ibid*., p. 38.

literature, "both kingship and priesthood contribute to the realization of the Renovation which requires their collaboration".[8]

I do not think we can affirm, with Jean de Menasce, that "the oft-repeated praise of the perfect Iranian kingship inspired by the Good religion and supporting it ... expresses the nostalgia for a bygone regime".[9] It would be more appropriate to say that it rather evokes "a mythical past" for one can always dream of as having been perfect.

The basic image through which this union between kingship and religion is expressed is that of *procreation*, as it appears in chapter 4 of the *Vizīdagīhā ī Zādsparam*.[10] It is explained there that the appearance of the Good Religion in the world, similar to the birth of a child, Spandarmad being the mother of the Religion, comes about even before the conversation of Zoroaster with Ohrmazd, that is to say, in the mythical times when Mazdaeism supposedly preceded the birth of the Founder. But more commonly, the image of this union is symbolised by two sisters or twins. Let us recall here some texts though they are quite well known. The *Letter of Tansar* mentions this theme in a unique way as follows:

"For Church and State were born of the one womb, joined together and never to be sundered. Virtue and corruption, health and sickness are of the same nature for both".[11]

In Masᶜūdī, Ardashir is supposed to have given the enthroned Šāpūr this advice that the author seems to attribute to Kārnāmag ī Ardašīr:[12]

"Know this, my son. Religion and kingship are two inseparable and interdependant sisters. For religion is the foundation of kingship and kingship its guardian. No construction not having a firm basis will escape collapse and whatever is not well guarded will perish."[13]

The interesting feature to observe here is the image of consanguinity to express the close link between religion and kingship. This image is even clearer in the *Testament of Ardashir*. For here not just sisters, but twins symbolise this intimate relationship.

8 *Ibid.*, p. 39. G. Gnoli, *La Persia nel Medioevo*, Roma 1971, p. 228, has also shown that the harmony between royalty and religion was nothing more than the transposition on a political level of the Zoroastrian conception of the Saviour.

9 J. de Menasce, *ibid.*, introduction p. 20–21.

10 See *Vichitakiha-i Zatsparam*, with Text and Introduction by B.T. Anklesaria, Bombay 1964, p. 44.

11 *The Letter of Tansar*, translated by M. Boyce, Roma 1968, p. 33–34.

12 See Masᶜūdī, *Les Prairies d'or*, French translation by Barbier de Meynard and Pavet de Courteille, revised and corrected by Ch. Pellat, Paris 1962, I p. 220: it is not clear whether Masᶜūdī drew his recommendations from the Kārnāmag. To my knowledge, they cannot be found there anyway, for after quoting this source, the author simply goes on to say "Here is a passage of the recommendations that time has spared ...".

13 *Ibid.*, p. 220.

"Know ye all that kingship and religion are twins, who can't exist one without the other. For Religion is the foundation of kingship and the king the guardian of Religion".
"Kingship has an absolute need of its foundation as Religion absolutely needs its protector. For the unprotected perishes and the unfounded collapses ...[14] and know ye all that the secret chief of Religion and the official master of the kingdom never coexist in a country if the religious chief doesn't contest over the power the chief of the kingdom is rightly invested with. For Religion is the foundation and kingship the pillar (of the kingdom) and the owner of the foundation has more right to the whole edifice than the owner of the pillar alone".[15]

These two texts are very similar and reflect the same tradition, both using the same image of an edifice[16], but in the second part of the text quoted above, allusion is also made to possible rivalry between the two powers, primacy nevertheless given to religion since it is the prop of the whole edifice. What is however to be remarked is the fact that the three texts refer *solely to the period of Ardashir*, that is to say, to a distant and legendary past of which the Arabo-Persians writers could not have preserved any guenuine traditions. My view is that it would not be an overstatement that we are here dealing with a *mythologisation* of an ideal conception of kingship, which was only translated into reality, in a different way of course, in subsequent Islam.

I would also like to draw a parallel of this twin conception with the old Indo-European ideology of the primeval twins, as construed for instance by Bruce Lincoln. In a recent work of his[17] he establishes in fact that the first king (*Yemo-) and the first priest (*Manu-) were twins and that, according to the Indo-European myth reconstructed in conjunction with the corresponding Indo-Iranian one, Manu killed his twin-brother thus performing the first sacrifice. I think that this image of twins in the Arabo-Persian historiography, as also in the Pahlavi literature, which associates in the same way both the role of warrior-king (State) and of priest (Church, Religion), can well be a mark of this same Indo-Iranian or Indo-European ideology. The true meaning of this unconscious and timeless memory is not so much the close alliance between both the civil and religious powers as their profound hostility and even their fight to death, which is amply testified by so

14 As quoted by M. Grignaschi, 'Quelques spécimens de la littérature sassanide', *Journal Asiatique* t. 254 (1966), p. 70 and note 10 p. 84: 'Al-Gazālī, the champion of moslem orthodoxy, has even considered it as a ḥadīṯ ...', which does indeed go to prove that such a conception belongs more to Islam than to Mazdeism.

15 M. Grignaschi, *ibid.*, p. 70.

16 Likewise, in the book of Ardā Vīrāz, chap. 2, 4, this holy priest is considered as a pillar supporting the house his seven sisters dwell in, according to a passage which has been misunderstood until now: 'Just like a roof with seven beams and a pillar beneath, if the pillar is withdrawn, the beams will collapse – so have we, the seven sisters, this only brother, who is our life and support'. (According to my new translation to be published by the A.D.P.F., Paris 1984.)

17 Bruce Lincoln, *Priests, Warriors and Cattle*, University of California Press, 1981, p. 87.

many events in human history.[18] It should follow from this significant similarity between the two myths that the Testament of Ardashir is the custodian of the most reliable tradition since it is the only tradition to mention explicitly the twins unless we are only faced with an adaptation to an ideology which could still be a living reality in the mind of the theologians.

If my interpretation of these texts is valid, it is still indispensable to examine if it is borne out by facts, that is to say, in a certain number of historical situations.

II. History of Relations between Religion and Kingship

We must first examine the question of the constitution of a state-Zoroastrianism in the 3rd century. For this reconstruction seems to be quite anachronic. Undoubtedly relying on the epigraphical writings of the great Magus Kirdīr (Kartir), many have given an enthusiastic acclaim to his views. He is said to have founded Fire Temples everywhere, persecuted with a notable success other religions and won favours from several kings, from Šāpūr I to Vahrām II. Without intending to minimize the work of this reformer (rather than a founder) of the Mazdean Church, one must not exaggerate his importance and the existence of a state religion in the 3rd century is not at all proved.[19] Years ago, G. Gnoli wisely concluded that "il mazdeismo non conquisto tutto d'un colpo la posizione privilegiata di religione dell'impero sassanide"[20], and "Nella creazione di una Chiesa di Stato gerarchicamente organizzata e di una ortodossia consacrata dalla codificazione di un canone dei testi sacri, . . . si ispirarono certamente all'illustre modello che offriva l'Occidente."[21] So, precisely this model of Byzantine Church did not become state-religion except gradually. Let us not forget that the conversion of Constantine in 325 and his proclamation of Christianity as the official religion did not *ipso facto* consecrate it as the state religion since, it is only at the end of the 4th century, at the death of Theodosius in 395, that the schism between the two parts of the Roman Empire was brought about. Even at this period, Constantinople had to contend with Antiochia which held an almost equal position as administrative and rival residence, from the religious point of view, up to the reign of Theodosius II (408–450). One is justified in thinking that only from

18 This is the meaning which can be given to the relentless determination of the Ayatollah Khomeiny to put the destitute and dying Shah to death – a pointless sacrifice as, according to Islamic tradition, he combined all powers within himself.

19 One can hardly even talk of a foundation of the Mazdean Church under the first Sasanians as G. Gnoli has done in *La Persia nel Medioevo*, Roma 1971, p. 243.

20 Gnoli, *ibid.*, p. 227.

21 Gnoli, *ibid.*, p. 231.

Justinian onwards in the 6th century did Christianity get equal rights. No doubt this was thanks to the dominant role played by the monastic communities, the prodigious development of which is visible everywhere in the 5th and 6th centuries from Egypt to Iran including Palestine.[22]

The evolution of the Mazdean church was, so it seems to me, if not comparable to that of Byzantine church, at all events as slow and perhaps even less favourable.

In a conference held recently at Collège de France[23], Gh. Gnoli demonstrated that the Sasanian Mazdaeism was *a national* religion whereas the great religions, which took root also in Iran, such as Christianity (Judaism before it), Manichaeism and Buddhism had an universalist appeal bent on a world conquest. It follows then, in my view, from this unquestionable difference that Mazdaeism found itself in an inferior position in relation to other religions, just as a national political party carries less weight than an "international" one.

Sasanian Mazdaeism had to face threats and rival forces, such as Christianity which was introduced in Iran from the 3rd century onwards[24], partly due to the royal policy massive deportation of Christians from neighbouring countries in Iran – Kirdīr did not favour this policy! – and to the birth of Manichaeism which developed rapidly thanks to the preaching based on *written texts* whereas this practice of written word was not yet prevalent with the Mazdeans as far as we know.[25] It is obvious that the persecutions of Kirdīr in the 3rd century did not

22 This development can be linked to the economic and demographic expansion which perhaps happened in the 5th and 6th centuries, while the first part of the Sasanian period (3rd–4th centuries) seems, on the contrary, to have been a time of regression and extreme poverty in the East. This is attested, in any case, for Palestine, if one refers to the study of Daniel Sperber, *Roman Palestine 200–400, The Land*, Crisis and Change in agrarian society as reflected in rabbinic sources, Bar-Ilan University, Ramat-Gan 1978. The third century, as the same author showed in a second volume with the subtitle 'Money and Prices', is a period of monetary devaluation and general economic decline, and, on the political level, of anarchic instability. In the 4th century, the situation shows a decided improvement, but there is little chance that it was much better in the Sassanian Empire, at the time of Shapur I. Unfortunately we still have too little information on this subject. However, according to Mas^cūdī, *Les Prairies d'or*, I p. 222, as Vahrām II give himself up to 'good cheer and pleasure', 'agriculture declined through lack of manpower; the courtiers had seized the principal domaines, and crops died out everywhere except on their lands . . ., the country went to rack and ruin, cultivated lands diminished and the finances of the state were exhausted'. This gloomy picture must correspond in some measure to a certain historical reality.

23 This is the last of a series of four lessons, given in April 1983, entitled 'Iran in the 3rd century between universalism and nationalism'. The whole work will be published in one of the volumes of the collection of the 'Travaux de l'Institut d'Etudes Iraniennes' of the 'Sorbonne Nouvelle', t. 11 (1984).

24 This is what emerges from the works of J. M. Fiey, cf. in particular *Communautés syriaques en Iran et Irak des origines à 1552*, Londres, Variorum Reprints, 1979.

25 I am still convinced that the mazdean doctors only understood the necessity of getting the Avesta

cause such disastrous effect for other religions as the triumphalist Magus would make us believe in his declarations taken *stricto sensu*. For the martyrdom of Mani did not at all lead to a rapid decline of the religion he founded. Thus a religion becomes persecutor when its dominant position is menaced or it wants to recover this position. It is rather to this second objective that the offensive policy of Kirdīr was geared.

Equally let us not forget that Kirdīr was "Mōbad of Ohrmazd" and "Judge of the whole empire." No organisation of provincial Mōbads directed by a Mōbadān Mōbad existed yet, since there was no more than one Mōbad.[26] Thus the religious functioning was not as *diversified* in its administrative cadre and hierarchy as the monarchy was with its King of Kings, provincial kings, governors of satrapies, viceroys and nobles, all divided into four large classes, and the military leaders. This system, no doubt inherited from the Arsacids, had been working for a long time. The Mazdean hierarchy was organised much later, not before the 5th century.[27] We should also bear in mind, as we have already observed, that Kirdīr has remained quite unknown to posterity and that, apart from his own inscriptions, no later text speaks about him except a brief mention of his name in the Paikuli inscription.[28]

The dearth of ancient religious monuments, Fire Temples, for the 3rd–5th centuries of the Sasanian period, even if it be an *a silentio* argument, does not give evidence in favour of any spectacular development of Mazdaeism.

Let us now turn to the question of relations between a Mazdean Church, which gradually becomes the official national church, and a highly centralised state under the absolute power of the King of Kings, with a long tradition of autocratic monarchy and of divine right, from the point of view of men at play. For both the civil and religious power is wielded by one single man at this juncture of the end of the Antiquity. During the 3rd century, it is Kirdīr who holds the absolute authority in the religious field, and his most significant act is perhaps the elimination of Mani whose personality seduced Šābuhr I. Later Mihr-Narseh holds the primacy over

and the Pahlavi commentaries and works down in writing from the moment that they noticed that Christianity and Manichaeism had acquired an unprecedented means of development and propaganda through the medium of the canon of their written sacred texts. Until then they had always relied on oral tradition alone.

26 As I have already written, if the title of *Mōbadān Mōbad* had already been in existence, Kirdīr would have no hesitation in stating it, and this title's only 'raison d'être' is when there are several Mōbads. Cf. my paper to the Jerusalem Colloquium 1980 'An outline of the religious functions under the Sasanians', to appear in the *JSAI*.

27 As shown in the Syriac documentation (Acts of the Persian Martyrs) and as noted already by Wikander.

28 Cf. now the new ed. of H. Humbach and Pr. O. Skjaervø, *The Sasanian Inscription of Paikuli*, Part 3.1, Restored text and translation, Wiesbaden 1983, p. 42: "Kirdēr the Mowbed of Ohrmazd'.

several kings and shows himself extremely intolerant of the Christians. His efforts to reconvert the Armenian Christians were doomed to failure. The history of this period is marked out by violent persecutions which bear witness to the obstacles Mazdaeism had to face in its effort to assert itself as the state religion.

The kings were not always relentless defendors of Mazdaeism against other religions. Šābuhr I was very attracted by Mani, but later it seems changed his mind, if we can reliably accept a manichaean text according to which he was cruel and violent.[29] Narseh, though noted for his piety, was not a regular faithful at the Fire Temples, according to Thaᶜālibī[30], and was very conciliatory to the Manichaeans and Christians.[31] Kavād was an active supporter of the Mazdakite movement[32] rather than an orthodox Mazdean. Xusrō I put an end to this subversive movement, but Xusrō II married the Christian Šīrīn and the Byzantine princess Maria, asserting thus his great personal independance of the mazdean matrimonial laws. The king, by reason of his absolute power, was far from being the unconditional supporter of Mazdaeism and its hierarchy[33], as the so-called alliance between the throne and the altar would make us believe. It is, on the contrary, in terms of *forces*, not always allied and often opposed, that the question of relations between the Church and the State should be considered. Even if the Mazdaean church was a winner in terms of power towards the end of the Sasanian period, Nestorianism in fact was always flourishing at this period in spite of persecutions and was well integrated in the Empire.[34] Therefore Mazdaeism should not be considered as a monolithic bloc. For different trends were at work within it, as for example, Zurvanism, even if the official religious administration was well rooted in each province, as is attested by the bullae at the end of this period.

29 Cf. W. Sundermann, *Mitteliranische manichäische Texte Kirchengeschichtlichen Inhalts*, Berliner Turfantexte XI, Berlin 1981, p. 107: 'In all lands he is called an evil-doer and a sinner' (sic).

30 H. Zotenberg, *Histoire des rois de Perse*, Paris 1900, p. 509–510.

31 Cf. M.-L. Chaumont, 'Les Sassanides et la christianisation de l'Empire iranien au IIIè siècle de notre ère', *Revue de l'Histoire des Religions* t.165, 1964, p. 200–201.

32 This movement existed even if one can doubt the historicity of Mazdak, as H. Gaube has done recently with sound arguments, 'Mazdak: historical reality or invention?', *Mélanges offerts à Raoul Curiel, Studia Iranica* 11 (1982), p. 111–122.

33 According to Masᶜūdī, *Les Prairies d'or*, I p. 236, Ohrmazd IV, by breaking the institution of the Mōbads, had destroyed the religious law, the ancestral traditions, the laws and customs of the Empire. And this is the end of the 6th century!

34 Cf. my paper at the Budapest Symposium 1980 (to be published) and my article 'Sceaux chrétiens d'époque sasanide', *Iranica Antiqua* vol. XV (1980), p. 299–314. See also W. Sundermann, 'Soziale Typenbegriffe altgriechischen Ursprungs in der altiranischen Überlieferung', *Soziale Typenbegriffe im alten Griechenland*, herausgegeben von E. Ch. Welskopf, Bd. 7, Berlin 1982, p. 14–38: in this article is assessed the importance of the Syriac language and culture as the vehicle in Iran of important concepts coming from the Greek world.

Finally we should not forget that the kings were not crowned by the Mōbad, but invested by the gods as depicted on the Sasanian bas-reliefs of Ardashir receiving the royal ring from Ahura Mazdā and Narseh from Anāhitā. The only exception handed to us by the Arabo-Persian writers is of king Vahrām Gōr crowned by the Mōbadān Mōbad. But this king is shrouded in so many legends that this account is not necessarily authentic and, of course, a single sparrow does not make a spring. For Firdousi, it is the king who crowns himself. This is certainly the genuine tradition, contrary to what Marie-Louise Chaumont has tried to demonstrate.[35] The king receives his power from the gods, not from the religious authority. Widengren went as far as to say that "the Sasanian kingship has a religious character of its own and is least marked by Zoroastrianism."[36]

All through the historical facts which I have cited, it appears then that the sacred alliance between kingship and religion is but a literary theme which developed mainly after the Sasanian period and, I would add, under Islamic influence which attempted, sometimes successfully, the symbiosis of these two powers, and which could even be linked with ancient Indo-Iranian mythology. The Mazdaeans theologians tried this in their active philosophical speculation, in this post-Sasanian period, solely to protect their religion from the dominant thrust of Islam. Those in power in Sasanian Iran, with their hierarchical structure, were so independant that this symbiosis, though apparently deeply desired, was not achieved.

35 Cf. his article 'Où les rois sassanides étaient-ils couronnés?', *Journal Asiatique* t. 252, 1964, p. 61–72. I do not think that the coronation in a fire-temple 'was a general rule with the Sasanians for the author, to prove it, uses 'the intimate alliance of the spiritual and the temporal which characterises this monarchy to the highest degree' (p. 71). I would like to show, on the contrary, the an-historical character of this alliance.

36 *Ibid.*, p. 352. G. Gnoli has also rightly affirmed, p. 249, that 'il re sassanide avesse un'autorità assoluta e completa anche negli affari della Chiesa, come dimostra il potere che aveva di fondare nuovi fuochi e di nominare i *mōbad* preposti alle varie province e lo stesso *mōbadān mōbad*'. The iconography shows it too, if one accepts the interesting interpretation by K. Tanabe of the complex of Taq-i Bustān, where the King of Kings is apparently depicted not only as presiding over the warrior function, but also as chief of the priest clan; see 'Iconographical and Iconological Study on the Larger Iwan at Taq-i Bustan', *Bulletin of the Okayama Orient Museum*, vol. 2 (1982), p. 61–113 (in Japanese).

* This English version of my paper I owe to my friend Dr. A. S. Yagappan, Paris, with some editorial changes.

LIST OF ABBREVIATIONS

AAAS	Les Annales Archéologiques Arabes Syriennes
ABL	R.F. Harper, Assyrian and Babylonian Letters, Chicago, 1892–1914
ADD	C.H.W. Johns, Assyrian Deeds and Documents, Cambridge, 1898–1923
AfO	Archiv für Orientforschung, Berlin–Graz
AION	Annali dell'Istituto Orientale di Napoli, Napoli
AnSt	Anatolian Studies
AOAT	Alter Orient und Altes Testament, Kevelaer–Neukirchen/Vluyn
ARAB	D.D. Luckenbill, Ancient Records of Assyria and Babylonia, New York, 1968 (reprint)
ARET	Archivi reali di Ebla – Testi, Missione Archeologica Italiana in Siria, Roma
ARI	A.K. Grayson, Assyrian Royal Inscriptions, Wiesbaden, 1976
ARM	Archives royales de Mari (= TCL 22–)
ARMT	Archives royales de Mari (Textes), Paris, 1950ff.
ASAE	Annales du Service des Antiquités de l'Égypte de Caire
AThANT	Abhandlungen zur Theologie des Alten und Neuen Testaments
BA	The Biblical Archaeologist, New Haven, Conn.
BAR	Biblical Archaeology Review
BARd	E.F. Campbell, Jr. (ed.), The Biblical Archaeologist Reader, 2, New York, 1964
BASOR	Bulletin of the American Schools of Oriental Research, Jerusalem – Bagdad – New Haven, Conn.
BdE	Bibliothèque d'Études Coptes, Institut Français d'Archéologie Orientale, Caire
BIN	Babylonian Inscriptions in the Collection of J.B. Nies, New Haven
BiOr	Bibliotheca Orientalis, Leiden
BO	s. BiOr
BZAW	Beiheft zur Zeitschrift für die alttestamentliche Wissenschaft, Berlin
CAD	The Assyrian Dictionary of the Oriental Institute of the University of Chicago, Chicago
CAH	Cambridge Ancient History
CISHAAN	Congrès International des Sciences Humaines en Asie et en Afrique du Nord
CML	G.R. Driver, Canaanite Myths and Legends, Edinburgh, 1956
CML^2	J.C.L. Gibson, Canaanite Myths and Legends, Edinburgh, 1978
CTA	A. Herdner, Corpus des tablettes en cunéiforme alphabétiques découvertes à Ras Shamra-Ugarit de 1929 à 1939, Paris, 1963
CTN	Cuneiform Texts from Nimrud, London, 1972ff.
DK	Dēnkard
DKM	Dēnkard ed. by D.M. Madan, I–II, Bombay, 1911

Ebla	G. Pettinato, The Archives of Ebla, an empire inscribed in clay, Garden City, 1981
Et. Trav.	Études et Travaux, Travaux de Centre d'Archéologie Méditerranéenne de l'Académie Polonaise des Sciences, Varsovie
HÄB	Hildesheimer Ägyptologische Beiträge
HUCA	Hebrew Union College Annual, Cincinnati, Oh.
Iran	R. Ghirshman, L'Iran dès origines à l'Islam, Paris, 1951
IUO	L. Cagni (ed.), *La lingua di Ebla*. Istituto Universitario Orientale Seminario di Studi Asiatici. Series Minor XIV, Napoli, 1981
JBL	Journal of Biblical Literature, Philadelphia, Pa.
JEA	The Journal of Egyptian Archaeology, London
JNES	Journal of Near Eastern Studies, Chicago, Ill.
JNSL	Journal of Northwest Semitic Languages, Leiden
JSS	Journal of Semitic Studies, Manchester
KRT	J. Gray, The Krt Text in the Literature of Ras Shamra, Leiden, 1964
KTU	M. Dietrich – O. Loretz – J. Sanmartín, Die keilalphabetischen Texte aus Ugarit, AOAT. 24/1, 1976
LC	J. Gray, The Legacy of Canaan, Leiden, 1965
LKK	H.L. Ginsberg, The Legend of Kiṅg Keret, New Haven, 1946
Management	M.W. Stolper, Management and Politics in Later Achaemenid Babylonia: New Textes from the Murašû Archive (Volumes I and II), Doctoral dissertation in the University of Michigan, Ann Arbor, 1974
MDAIK	Mitteilungen des Deutschen Archäologischen Instituts in Kairo, Berlin
MEE	Materiali epigrafici di Ebla, Napoli
MFUL	A. van Selms, Marriage and Family Life in Ugaritic Literature, London, 1954
MKT	J. Aistleitner, Die mythologischen und kultischen Texte aus Ras Schamra, Budapest, 1959
NSR	H. Genge, Nordsyrisch-südanatolische Reliefs I–II, København, 1979
OrAn	Oriens Antiquus, Roma
OrNS	Orientalia, Nova Series, Roma
PEQ	Palestine Exploration Quarterly, London
PHPKB	J.A. Brinkman, A Political History of Post-Kassite Babylonia 1158–722 B.C., Rome, 1968
PLMU	C.H. Gordon, Poetic Legends and Myths from Ugarit, Berytus 25 (1977), pp. 5–133
POTT	D.J. Wiseman (ed.), Peoples of Old Testament Times, London, 1973
PRU	Le Palais Royal d'Ugarit publié sous la direction de C.F.A. Schaeffer, Paris
RBI	Rivista Biblica. Associazione biblica Italiana, Brescia
RdE	Revue d'Égyptologie, Caire
RLA	Reallexikon der Assyriologie, Berlin
RSP	Ras Shamra Parallels, I. II. III. L.R. Fischer, editor, AnOr. 49, 1972–1981
RStOR	Rivista degli Studi Orientali, Roma

SBH	G. Reisner, Sumerisch-babylonische Hymnen nach Tontafeln griechischer Zeit, Berlin, 1896
SEb	Studi Eblaiti, Roma
SPDS	T. Ishida (ed.), Studies in the Period of David and Solomon and other Essays, Tokyo, 1982
St.Or.	Studia Orientalia, Helsinki
Stories	M.D. Coogan, Stories from Ancient Canaan, Philadelphia, 1978
TCL	Musée du Louvre. Départment des Antiquités Orientales. Textes cunéi formes, Paris
TEBR	F. Joannès, Textes économiques de la Babylonie récente (Etudes Assyriologiques, Cah. no. 5), Paris, 1982
THAT	Theologisches Handwörterbuch zum Alten Testament. I–II. München, 1971–1976
TO	A. Caquot–M. Sznycer–A. Herdner, Textes Ougaritiques, T. I: Mythes et légendes, Paris, 1974
UET	Ur Excavations, Texts, London, 1928ff.
UF	Ugarit-Forschungen, Kevelaer–Neukirchen/Vluyn
Ug	Ugaritica I–VII, Paris, 1939–1978
UL	C.H. Gordon, Ugaritic Literature (= Scripta Pontificii Instituti Biblici 98), Rome, 1949
USHK	W. Orthmann, Untersuchungen zur späthethitischen Kunst, Bonn, 1971
UT	C.H. Gordon, Ugaritic Textbook (= AnOr. 38), Rome, 1965
VT	Vetus Testamentum, Leiden
WO	Die Welt des Orients, Göttingen
YOS	Yale Oriental Series, Babylonian Texts
ZA	Zeitschrift für Assyriologie und Vorderasiatische Archäologie, Berlin
ZÄS	Zeitschrift für Ägyptische Sprache und Altertumskunde
ZAW	Zeitschrift für alttestamentliche Wissenschaft, Berlin